M000074266

SIGNIFICANCE AND MEANS OF SELF-KNOWLEDGE

SIGNIFICANCE AND MEANS OF SELF-KNOWLEDGE

TUSHAR CHOKSI

Advaya Press

Copyright © 2019, 2020, 2021 by Tushar Choksi

All rights reserved. This book or any portion thereof may not be reproduced or used in any manner whatsoever without the express written permission of the publisher except for the use of brief quotations in a book review.

Printed in the United States of America

Third Edition 2021

First edition published 2019. Second edition published 2020.

ISBN: 978-1-7373976-1-8

Advaya Press

अध्यात्मज्ञाननित्यत्वं तत्वज्ञानार्थदर्शनम् |

एतज्ज्ञानमिति प्रोक्तमज्ञानं यदतोऽन्यथा ||

I BOW DOWN TO

SRINATHJI (ISHVARA) WITH LOVE,

THE INDWELLING SELF OF ALL

CONTENTS

FOREWORD

Who has not experienced suffering in this world? It's our personal experience in day-to-day life. In some moments, we are happy and in the very next moment we feel sadness, pain, or sorrow. Suffering is like our shadow that does not leave us. This is the fundamental problem of human life. Our life and choices therein are driven by wanting, becoming, trying, and tasting to get rid of this suffering. Human beings have freedom over desires, and desires are endless, but capacity is limited! This leads to the problem of unfulfillment and inadequacy that eventually leads to unhappiness, sorrow, and limitedness. A person feeling limited can never be secure or happy. The very struggle of achieving happiness remains lifelong but never fulfils. This is not wisdom. It is a sign of immaturity. A wise man knows how to become free from this vicious cycle of suffering. A wise man knows how to think, act, and behave maturely and knows the basis for the steadiness of the intellect and mind. The basis of this wisdom is rooted in ancient Indian scriptures: the Vedantic text. The Sacred texts are composed of Vedas, Upanishads, Bhagavat Geeta and Brahma Sutra. It brings a perspective of universal oneness and removes ignorance about self. Once Vedantic vision is unfolded, man can achieve everlasting peace, happiness, bliss, and security. Suffering can be eliminated. This is the grand promise of this wisdom.

This book discovers the connection between self-knowledge and happiness, and self-ignorance and suffering with utmost clarity. This book does an excellent job of bringing this connection to us, like removing the blindfold from a blindfolded man. It takes us on a journey of self-knowledge from Jiva to Bhakta and ultimately to Ishvara, the self of all. This universal wisdom is not something one is going to stumble upon. It is also beyond the comprehension of common men.

A Human being is pure by nature. No baby is ever born with any sort of impurity of mind whatsoever. No parents want their children to follow bad paths. Basic ethics and values that govern most humans on earth are well established. It is there in every religion or theology and is the same. So then why are there conflicts, differences, and unhappiness? The problem is that we have confined ourselves to a certain dogma, sect, religion, or theology without understanding its root connection to Ishvara.

We have taken them at face value and are not seeing them as a stepping ladder that can take us closer to the ultimate. Without understanding this connection, one can never become free from sorrow. Subjectivity can never be reduced. We have a subjective definition of success in terms of material belonging, but can it give lasting happiness? Can it remove our suffering forever? What is true success in life? What is successful living or what is a fulfilling life? dharma, or religion, shows us the path, but the journey only starts with that! It cannot be the final destination unless we have found answers to these hard problems of suffering, sorrow, and unhappiness.

This book does an excellent job of unfolding this connection to one's life, one's dharma, one's religion, one's theology, and one's personal god. It unfolds this grand Vedantic vision in simple yet terse language. These are everyone's problems and without this understanding, life remains a struggle. This book brings an amazing clarity on what it means to be human, what my role and the ultimate goal is, who I really am, how I am connected to the universe, what is the role of Bhakti, family life, dharma, and meditation in my life and connects them to the universal grand Vedantic vision that has the greatest power to uplift any human being.

This book is for every human being who repeatedly goes through this journey of happiness and suffering like the two sides of a coin. This is the story of you, me, and every human being who feels like a puppet to our feelings and emotions, and who wants to understand our true nature, and who want to remove this ignorance to bring lasting happiness.

The author is a well learned and respected Vedantic scholar, highly educated Software Engineer by profession, and an avid student of Vedantic scriptures. I have known him personally for many years and have benefited greatly from his command and succinct clarity on this subject. His subject expertise comes from many years of personal and focused study of texts, commentaries, and Bhasya's from many well-known Acharya's and gurus from the Shankar tradition, and from following it in his own personal life. He has been a student of the Swadhyay movement since childhood. The Swadhyay parivar (loosely analogous to "organization") devoted to bringing Vedic thoughts and its application in our life in an applied philosophy form. Swadhyay is a silent but singing revolution inspired by late Pujya Pandurang Shastri from Mumbai. I came in close connection with the author through the same means and it blossomed into a very close and personal bonding influenced by the shared common interest in Vedanta and especially because of his intense love and clarity on these thoughts.

This is a book for all common men who want to unfold this connection and grand wisdom about ultimate reality in their daily life and get rid of personal misery or suffering. This book plays the role of the torch. With its light, one can uncover the path to reach the ultimate goal of human life. As someone famously said, we are not human beings in search of a spiritual experience; we are spiritual beings immersed in a human experience. Let us unfold this powerful vision and discover our true self. May God give all of us bliss, grace, and the capacity to go through this journey. Om Shanti Shanti Shanti!

Chirag Desai

Bachelor of Engineering (Computer Science)

San Jose, CA

PREFACE

I was always convinced that human life is more about quality than quantity. At the end of the day, how happy and safe, we are as a human being matters to us most. Every human being wants absolute happiness and safety, which determines one's quality of life. This book is a serious investigation into that which everybody ultimately wants. It answers every human being's question of how to improve one's quality of life, for which we are trying so hard every day and for our whole life.

This book describes human evolution, or the journey of an individual, from suffering to relatively happy, and from a relatively happy to absolutely happy and safe in the light of Vedant. Of course, in order to improve one's quality of life, one has to put in some effort. This book declares that the effort has to be in a spiritual direction. It proves that as human beings, our happiness and safety depend upon self-knowledge, how we see ourselves, or a true under-standing of human personality, which is the single root cause for being happy and safe. Everything else we try that is not in the direction of self-knowledge and spirituality is just a pain killer; it can only temporarily solve human issues. Due to our neglect of looking in the direction of self, consciousness, or God, and always finding a material solution, we inevitably stay in the same place of human suffering. Endlessly following the urges of mind and body and never recognizing the true self of a human being is the recipe of human suffering.

The initial chapters of the book establish the connection between self-ignorance and human suffering. The topic that I am trying to discuss here is not only about self-knowledge itself, but its significance and connection to human suffering as Vedant sees it. If Vedant and human experience are understood properly, it has the ability to alleviate and remove human suffering and to recover total happiness and safety for a human being.

Progressively, the book shows that progress in self-knowledge is progress in the quality of everyday human life. The book includes contemplation, which will be very useful to all.

To evolve or develop ourselves and recover our highest quality of life, or being, requires some means or aids for advancing on the path of self-knowledge. As we all know, stable progress does not happen in one stroke. The middle of the book describes such Vedantic tools, their purpose, and the value it provides in terms of human evolution.

By analyzing and understanding the nature of an individual in the light of Vedant, we can get rid of suffering and sorrow clinging to us. A few chapters following the means of self-knowledge explain the self-knowledge by in-depth analysis of the nature of an individual based on the field and the knower of the field discrimination of the *Bhagavad Gita*.

The last chapters praise self-knowledge and its sacredness because of the value it provides to human beings. We are human beings. We enjoy and become sad, but we have an intellect and Vedant to reach our ultimate destiny.

Our progress as human beings becomes stagnant and our lives become robotic and mechanical by our constant denial of the self, consciousness, or God. This book is thus a very brief attempt to achieve our human goal of immortality, total understanding of ourselves, and the truth of existence.

ACKNOWLEDGMENTS

My parents built in me the goal of being a good, virtuous human being, and they gave me the goal of spirituality. My father, Mahendrabhai, and mother, Kokilaben, both were teachers. I will always remain indebted to both my parents for raising me in a loving, virtuous, and self-disciplined environment. The importance of moral values, education, and character was their gift to create a good human being out of me. I went to Bhagavad Katha with my mother and father regularly. My grandparents taught me various stotras of Shrinathji, who is our deity. My grandparents always used to take me to nearby temples in our town on foot, and we used to do Darshan of Shrinathji. I did not know that, unconsciously, these gifts built love and respect for Ishvara in my heart, which would result in my quest for reality using Vedant in later years. I cannot repay the debt to my grandparents and parents, even if I try many lives. How can I forget my beloved younger sister,

Rajeshwari, who always accompanied me to all my activities? Even today, she is my best companion. My father put me and my sister in school, where Bhagavad Gita was recited regularly. My first introduction to Bhagavad Gita occurred in primary school, where Mother Gita was in the center of the hall. Since then, the Bhagavad Gita has kept the place of my spiritual mother. The school principal, Gitaben, was very generous and loving to me and she always inspired me to live a spiritual and disciplined life.

My mother's cousin, Mr. Gopalbhai chokshi, or Gopalmama (Vadodara), was the one who really concretized a spiritual goal in my life. I can say that he has initiated me on the path of spirituality when I was very young. I cannot forget him throughout my life. All the necessary groundwork, such as reading scriptural books, participating in cultural activities, and attending spiritual talks, was regularly performed with him. He introduced me to Swadhyaya, which is a spiritual family-based activity of revered and beloved Shastri Pujya Pandurang Athvale, who we affectionately call Dadaji.

When in college, I was inspired by Shri Ramkrishna and Vivekananda's works. I frequently visited their centers and studied in-depth the great people whose influence turned me into a serious seeker of spirituality. The Swadhyaya activity gave me the platform that I needed for spiritual and human development ever since I was a child and continuing on as a young and intelligent person. Dadaji explained all the intricacies of Vedantic philosophy centered on the Bhagavad Gita. His simple video lectures are filled with the love of Ishvara and the pravachans are inspiring different Bhakti based cultural and spiritual activities. I was graced by Dadaji. When I was very young, Jitubhai Patel, Mahadevbhai tewar, and Gopalmama personally took care of me about what I used to read, think, and feel. I do not have words to thank Dadaji for providing me Ishvara's grace and love as a Guru. What I can say further? I was spiritually nurtured and felt the love of Ishvara, with fellow swadhyayees. My head simply bows down to Dadaji with gratitude, humility, respect, and love.

The spirituality that was developing in me did not become a concrete experience until I came in touch with the Vedantic lectures of Swami Dayananda Saraswati of Arsha Vidya tradition. Even though I was in touch with Shankar bhashya on Upanishads since I was in college, I knew something was still lacking in my knowledge and experience. After studying Shankar bhashya commentaries of Swami Dayananda's tradition, I found the missing link. I found myself dumb here due to the lack of words for the Swamiji. I sat before his samadhi at the Rishikesh ashram and paid respect to him.

I want to acknowledge my gorgeous, caring, and loving wife, Yamini, intelligent, dedicated, and lovely son Atri, charming, determined, and lovely daughter Charvi, vigorous, smart, and loving daughter-in-law Jinal for their continuous loving support for me. Spirituality cannot grow without loving support from the family. Thanks to my son, daughter, and the wife for eagerly and continuously supporting me in the direction of spirituality for many years. I want to especially thank Atri and Jinal for their help in the publication of this book.

I acknowledge Chirag Desai for his kind comments in the foreword as well as his precious friendship and love for me. Naturally, I cannot acknowledge everybody here that played a part in developing Vedantic vision in me as described in Shruti. So, let me take a shortcut now and acknowledge Ishvara, the self of all, with love and respect and without whose grace nothing would have been possible.

Part One

SIGNIFICANCE OF SELF-KNOWLEDGE

Chapter One

STORY OF A BLINDFOLDED MAN

a story occurs in *Chandogya Upanishad*[1] where a man is kidnapped from his village, blindfolded, and left in a dense forest. The forest did not have a human population and is inhabited by wildlife like tigers, lions, and snakes. Due to his eyes being covered, the man had no sense of direction and didn't know where to go. Finding himself helpless, he started screaming for help. Fortunately, a stranger passed by after sometime. The stranger saw him and removed his bandage. The relieved man told his story to the rescuer. He told him how he was brought here after being robbed and asked for directions to go back to his village. The compassionate stranger gave him directions and informed him of various signposts along the way. By following the stranger's directions and without getting distracted along the way, the man reached his home in the village.

How does this story relate to us? Let us check our position as a human being. We try to educate ourselves, get a good job, get insurance, get married, have kids, make friends, get status, get money, and get power. But getting something and getting rid of something always continues without ever being able to complete and secure ourselves. As human beings, we are highly insecure and incomplete; as a result, we are constantly looking for security and happiness. We try to look for security and happiness from wherever we get, like it has been robbed by some dacoits. We are subject to suffering from pain, pleasure, attachment, and aversion. Our relationships do not work out, and objects elude us. We constantly worry about acquiring, removing, and maintaining necessary objects and relationships. As soon as we see our first gray hair, we become worried. We constantly fear disease, death, and hence try to become deathless. Our life is a life of continuous becoming to become perfect. We become exhausted and tired by the continuous search for happiness and securing ourselves. But happiness and security remain ever elusive. We constantly try to remove our limitations of body, mind, and intellect as we are embodied. We find that we are subjected to anxiety, loneliness, anger, hatred, and depression. We are happy for a moment and suddenly sad if some thought disturbs us. Sorrow is ever clinging to human life. These mental demonic tendencies are the wild animals in the story that are always ready to devour a human being. When we honestly look at the human situation, we must admit that human existence is vulnerable and subject to *Samsara*.

We work hard to enjoy the bites of happiness. In order to repeatedly enjoy these bites of fleeting joy, we work again to adjust situations, objects, and relations to be conducive of promised pleasure or satisfaction. Thus, karma and bhoga forms the cycle of *Samsara* for us and we can't find a way out. We try to secure us which is inherently insecure and try to make us happy which is by nature unhappy or incomplete.

Above is the honest big picture of every human being going through various experiences and tribulations of life. Although a human being is relatively happy and free compared to other species of creation, this story is meant for taking us from relative happiness to absolute happiness. Now, the story narrated in the first paragraph will make sense to a man of discrimination. The story of a blindfolded man is a story of every human being as every human being is existentially subjected to death and a sense of incompleteness. Ok, what about the eye bandage in the story? Only a human being is provided with the most powerful faculty of intellect in the creation and has the highest capacity or potentiality to fulfil himself. By the same token, human intellect is subjected to ignorance or not-knowing until it gets educated. This ignorance is not so much of a problem as long as it is ignorance about other than oneself. However, a special type of ignorance called self-ignorance forms the root cause of *Samsara* and acts like a blindfold to a human being until it is removed. This self-ignorance, or avidya, forms the third basic limitation of human existence following incompleteness and fear of death. In fact, avidya is the root limitation out of which the other two limitations spring into existence.

Self-ignorance is an ignorance of the real nature of a human being, about one's own self-identity. As soon as a human being takes birth, avidya comes with it. The greatest limitation a human being has is not knowing oneself, in its true sense, as it is. Each one of us has different misconstrued ideas about who we are that are born out of our own erroneous and ignorant thinking. We acquire every other objective knowledge correctly through its right means of knowledge to avoid confusion and error. For example, if one wants to become a doctor, one goes to medical school and works hard to achieve certified knowledge. But in the case of knowledge about oneself, we either assume or entertain some ideas about oneself, and never think that knowledge of oneself should be improved through the right means of knowledge. Self-ignorance is a subjective limitation like the blindfolded man, and therefore must be pointed out by something external to the self; Then, one has to inquire and learn. In the story, the stranger who is not blindfolded is such a means of knowledge as Shruti, Vedant, or guru is in our life. The only one who has mastered self-knowledge through the right means of knowledge can remove self-ignorance. Generally, we spend our life in the effort of survival, comfort, and may be in an organization based on our beliefs. Few ask basic questions about 'Who am I', 'What am I', or what is the real nature of that which I call upon as myself centered on which everything revolves. Even fewer ask these basic questions in the light of Vedant, Shruti, or Brahma Vidya, whose main topic is this only.

The story goes that man reaches his home after following the directions given by the compassionate stranger. The key idea that runs with the story is that the problem of a human being as a samsari is centered on oneself. By educating oneself through the right means of knowledge and a teacher, one can reach fulfilment in this life. A human child takes birth with intellect, gathers some objective knowledge based on the surroundings, but has no validated knowledge of itself. To achieve the fulfilment that every human being is seeking, it is important that one understands that self-ignorance is a blindfold that can and needs to be removed. When we say the three limitations are existential, it means they only cover oneself, apparently; they are not really there in the true self of a human being. Our prime effort should be to acquire self-knowledge through a valid means of knowledge and through a qualified teacher. Human life means experiences, duties and relations to reach absolute happiness and immortality.

The story introduced the topic of self-knowledge and made a very important point about human life. We need to dig further to understand self-ignorance as the cause of *Samsara* and its effects in our life to justify the effort of self-knowledge, moksha, or liberation in life itself.

---

1. 6.14

Chapter Two

JIVA AND SUFFERING

*L*et me start by defining myself as an individual person. As soon as I open my eyes, as an individual, I encounter another entity called the world. A definition of the relationship between me and the world is required because the world is there and I am here – a human endowed with intellect and body is here. I am an individual entity; hence I am separate from the world, and the world is separate and independent from me. I am separate from God or totality. As I am endowed with the doership, I earn through work and enjoy the results of my work. In other words, I am a Jiva, as my self-identity is based on body and intellect. I am the proud enjoyer and a doer. I achieve money, status, family, power and enjoy them. In order to enjoy, I achieve what I want to enjoy in life. I know, I do, and I enjoy. I am a responsible person and aware of my rights.

Let us examine how the dualistic knowledge of Jiva/individual, that I am separate from the world and God, and the world and God is separate from me, is the cause of suffering. Because I am separate from the world, I need to continuously protect myself from the world or others. It is comprehensible while it's for self-preservation. However, I can exploit others or vice versa. We see individuals exploiting others in society for profit. Because alienation from the total defines the individual, he is always highly insecure. This insecurity pushes Jiva to do almost anything because the insecurity causes fear for his survival. The mental attitude resulting from a strict sense of individuality is of always defending oneself from the world, dominating the world, or remaining away from the world. Various desires for objects will spring up because of Jiva's inherent sense of incompleteness. Jiva can transgress the laws also to satisfy his cravings. If Jiva is unable to achieve the objects of his liking, he will become angry. Anger will cause Jiva to forget his status as a human and degrade himself to animal-like behaviors. The same is true with greed, lust and attachment. Disharmony and conflicts with the environment are quite natural in a Jiva. Jiva, afflicted with the strong sense of individuality, lives in constant fear, restlessness, anxiety and tension because the border between himself and the world is very thick. As a Jiva, self-interest will pervade his mentality. I don't care. I need not take care of anybody or I will take care of another only for any self-interest. There is no other reason Jiva can find to help or take care of the world.

How I behave with my fellow beings and environment differs from Jiva to Jiva. The behaviors range from uncontrolled to unconnected and dry. An individual is almost always in competition with other individuals due to his separateness and always lives in fear of failure.

A set of mental complexes make up Jiva. For example, I am fat; I am blonde; I hate myself or I hate the world; I am an angry person; I am better than him or he is better than me; I am handsome or ugly; I am less achieved. Inferiority and superiority complexes are very common in Jiva's personality. I can never stop forming different mental complexes as a Jiva. If these complexes become deeply rooted and hardened, mental disorders will be created. Feeling of loneliness is another rampant problem plaguing society that also has its roots from a highly individualistic notion of life. A person can feel lonely even in the midst of a crowd. Non-self-acceptance, self-dissatisfaction, and a sense of insignificance will always survive in the background of the Jiva. This self-dissatisfaction of being small will result in a life of continuous running to become bigger and better than what I am now.

Jiva's mind is always bouncing between the conflicting emotions of strong attachment and aversion. As Jiva is alienated from total, he locates happiness in external objects, persons, and situations, and always falls short of complete and permanent happiness at all times. Jiva tries to achieve objects, persons and situations that are supposed to make him happy. Jiva creates attachment to the objects he likes and creates disdain for objects he does not like. This dislike creates disharmony with the environment resulting in anger, frustration, fear and hatred in his unconscious. The pressure of attachment and aversion makes an individual transgress the moral values of truth, honesty, integrity, non-violence, kindness and service. Jiva is mainly a doer and enjoyer. Jiva will gather guilt due to some actions performed by him. Jiva will also gather hurt because of some unexpected responses from the world. Jiva's unconscious becomes heavier and heavier, resulting in an unpleasant and pressured state of mind and character. It's as if a garbage bag is filled up with trash, but there is no dumpster where it can be emptied. As an individual's responses are governed more and more by his unconscious, his responses to external events will become more and more tense. When a light interaction of Jiva with the world creates an intense reaction from Jiva, it is because of being filled up unconscious.

As a Jiva, I am a personality consisting of desires, thoughts, feelings, actions and sensations.

The root of what I desire, think, feel, act and sense is found to be Jivahood or one's knowledge about oneself as a limited entity. The basis of mind-body make-up is pervaded by Jivahood. I am limited by the mind-body complex as a human being. Suffering is then an experiencer ruffled by an unwanted continuous stream of desires, thoughts, feelings, actions and sensations. Jiva suffers helplessly from not being able to resolve or get rid of unwanted modifications of his mind-body.

Suffering is an unwanted pattern of experiences or memory that is unavoidable. Jiva is a samsari because his experience comprises a wanted and unwanted mix of mental modifications and patterns. Jiva cannot avoid unwanted ones and keep only the good ones because both constitute his personality. As a result, sleeping pills are a relief to many human beings. In the worst-case, most unfortunately, a human being does suicide to escape from his suffering, which is always avoidable. This is *Avidya* or self-ignorance which forms the root cause of *Samsara*.

Even if a person is well-educated, becoming a doctor, a lawyer, or an engineer, is a CEO of a company, is high up in politics, military, or business, earns a hefty amount of money, has family and friends, he still lives an inner life of Jiva which demands constant evolution to perfect happiness without a trace of sorrow. Such a highly educated person can still be full of hatred, anger, anxiety, depression, stress, not cooperative, hence unhappy and full of suffering. The fact about a human being is that one has to face oneself. The fact is that one has to first face one's own fear, anxiety, stress, anger and disappointment. How can one face oneself without any self-knowledge?

An individual's experience is a reflection of how one cognizes oneself. For example, if one's personality is to constantly complain, then one strongly believes that the world and oneself are separate entities. The world does not interpret itself, nor tell me anything about it. One's intellect interprets the world based on one's current knowledge. Strong dualistic knowledge about self and the world tantamount to suffering. An unhappy experience means one is away from the truth. Experience of what takes place in one's mind-body can be improved by self-knowledge. Self-knowledge removes mental suffering and reduces physical suffering to its minimum level of mere sensations. A dualistic yardstick by which one measures and interprets one's experience leads to suffering. It is not that the world, or oneself, is bad or good. Suffering is an indication to improve on self-knowledge.

Even though we have intellect as a human being, we can't avoid suffering. The reason is that we have neglected something very basic and essential to being a human. We neglect self-knowledge and are busy eating, drinking and merrymaking. Our intellect has never looked into the direction of the self, which it should look first and foremost. It is like forgetting the supporting earth on which one is standing, thinking one is standing by oneself without any support, and continuing to believe that even though an earthquake happens. It is a gross error of not inquiring and not paying attention to self that results in suffering.

One never asks questions like 'what is the true self of a human being?' or 'what is my relation to God and the world?'. One verse in the *Isavasya Upanishad*[1] states that the slayer of self goes to or lives in a world of darkness, non-divinity, and gloom bereft of peace, happiness, love, and understanding. This two sentence verse directly connects suffering of a human being to his neglect of self-knowledge. If one considers questions of self-inquiry such as 'who am I?' Or 'what am I?' is unnecessary, it's like a thirsty fish which badly needs water while swimming in water boasts, why should I inquire about water?. Questions of self-inquiry are not abstract questions to ask and reserved for philosophers, but fundamental questions that every human should ask because it is related to one's happiness. If one is fully convinced of the importance of these questions, then one should be serious enough to inquire with the guidance of Shruti, Vedant, or a qualified teacher of Vedant to get to the right knowledge of the self. Self-knowledge is capable of transporting Jiva from relative happiness and insecurity to another shore of the sea of *Samsara* of absolute peace, happiness and immortality. *Chandogya Upanishad*[2] says that the knower of the self crosses sorrow.

Human experience seems to be limited, but can be improved. Vedant improves the human experience by first turning one's attention to the self and then by restoring one's self as it is. Moksha, liberation in life, is thus defined as recovering oneself as it is. Vedant is a systematic, cognitive approach to show one unity of self, God and the world. The purpose of this work is to find enough reasons and connections to prepare for the efforts in the direction of self-knowledge to ultimately restore our happiness and freedom. Shortcomings inherent in Jiva are removed when we come in touch with our true self, which is by nature ever present, consciousness, and peaceful.

Let us say that one takes up this endeavor of self-knowledge because of its significance. Let us see the steps to progress and how ignorance about self's real nature is gradually removed.

Learning self-knowledge happens in the same way as learning chemistry, physics, math or computer science. One gradually becomes aware of what one really is. One needs to become an undergraduate first, followed by a graduate. As Jiva progresses in self-knowledge, he becomes Bhakta/devotee first, then finds his oneness with Ishvara. We are not only concerned with self-knowledge itself in this work, but its impact on one's life. Let's explore what a Bhakta/devotee is and how he sees the world and God.

---

1. 3
2. 7.1.3

Chapter Three

BHAKTA AND EVER-CONNECTEDNESS

a Bhakta or Devotee is an individual whose self-knowledge has progressed because of his spiritual practices. Bhakta sees himself as never separate from Ishvara, the Lord of the universe, with attributes. His self-identity consists of an individual who can never ever be separated from the total, essence, or the only reality of the universe that we experience, like a tree rooted in the ground. His understanding of self is that of a baby playing in the motherly background of reality with which he is intimately connected. He is completely dependent on the background and his essence is one with Ishvara, which is the same reality of everything else. In this way, Bhakta is ever connected to the essence of the universe: Ishvara. Bhakta knows that universal self-hood is the nature of all things, including himself. Bhakta sees the world as a world-form Ishvara to which he belongs and intimately tied with love. Thus Bhakta sees that all relations are intimate, and it is the Ishvara who is intimacy in the form of all relations. Just like a wave in the ocean is an integral part of the ocean, Bhakta considers the world the lap of Ishvara, his mother, on which he plays and is intimately ever connected to. Bhakta's strength is his knowledge about his connection with Ishvara. He has knowledge of Ishvara as an indweller and as one closest to him. Bhakta is a life of belonging and commitment to Ishvara.

Let us examine how self-knowledge of the intimate connection between I and the world creates an excellent human being called Bhakta. Since human society consists of individuals, if individuals have such self-knowledge, the whole society and world becomes heaven on the earth. *Bhagavad Gita*[1] explains the relation between Bhakti and Ishvara in two verses. Bhakta, due to his recognition of Ishvara, becomes always conforming to the universal order of right and wrong, i.e., the dharma while interacting with the world. Rather than acting in the self-centered way, Bhakta acts naturally based on dharma or moral order. Moral values of sympathy, compassion, truthfulness, love, non-violence are not created in a Bhakta one by one, but at once due to his Bhakti to Ishvara. A person may be a criminal, but once he recognizes Ishvara and becomes a Bhakta, he starts behaving with moral values. He sees Ishvara in the form of moral values or the order in creation. Because creation is not separate from Ishvara, all moral values come from him. Bhakta recognizes moral values and acts conforming to dharma naturally as part of his devotion.

A person violates the moral order because of being highly insecure. On the other hand, a Bhakta's connection with Ishvara makes him secure in his essence. Bhakti re-orients a rights-oriented person to a duty and love oriented person. Bhakti is the best recipe for creating the best individuals, society, country, and the world.

Now let us take the biggest problem of human suffering and see how Bhakti solves it. All suffering and human problems are rooted in alienation of Jiva with Ishvara, in a separate person. Jiva becomes secure and happy once the alienation is corrected with the self-knowledge of Bhakti: Ishvara is his maker and the material. Jiva is not and never was separate from Ishvara. He does not see everything other than himself as outside and separate, but instead within and intimate. He is fulfilled because of his seeing of Ishvara, the common essence of himself and the world, as his father, mother, and the source. His emotions get the eternal therapy provided by a mother and father. His thoughts stem from security and assurance. His acts become constructive. He accepts himself and the world as it is and totally. He knows that Ishvara is with him as his partner and will never leave him. His will, thoughts, feelings, and actions become harmonious and center on love and knowledge of Ishvara. Bhakta restores the harmony of his body and mind by removing the sense of alienation. For example, if Bhakta has a habit of smoking, he will grow out of that compulsion of habit by understanding that it irritates the indwelling Ishvara who is fullness and wholeness in nature.

Such a Bhakta also restores the harmony between himself and the world. A Bhakta creates self-dignity and reverence for the world due to his feeling-knowledge of nearness and relatedness of Ishvara. Bhakta clearly knows that his self-dignity and self-confidence comes from Ishvara and not from any of his possessions like position, fame, degree, money, power or other objects. How can a Bhakta become obsessed and helpless from objects when dependence on objects is removed? Bhakta becomes carefree with respect to objects and creates intimacy with all living beings. As his Bhakti deepens, Bhakta starts developing the divine virtues of compassion, forgiveness, peace, selfless love, and selfless work. His actions, emotions, and thoughts start getting an impulse from Bhakti as opposed to selfishness, which is the recipe of suffering.

Bhakta is relieved of loneliness, a major cause of suffering, as a result of his understanding that Ishvara is always with him. Fear of death is the fear of going to an unknown place. Bhakta understands and trusts completely that he is going back home to the source. Thus, fear of death is removed. How can the lovely son of Ishvara hate or create negativity about himself?

Bhakta accepts his limitations naturally because he identifies as belonging to wholeness and is not himself a limited entity.

He lives with the pride of belonging to the fullness, and this ever connectedness allows him to accept his short-comings. Bhakta is a humble person. He learns to pardon himself and creates a path of development from Jiva to Ishvara. Ishvara acts as an altar of Bhakta where Bhakta can sacrifice his limitations like anger, hatred, greed, attachment, and delusion. These are major causes of suffering which are removed, and thus, the suffering of Jiva is relieved. He becomes loving, peaceful, happy; he acts with love of Ishvara, and he acts according to dharma. Just like a pregnant woman in her every part-of-being feels, thinks, and acts amidst the presence of her unborn child, Bhakta knows, feels, thinks, wills, and acts amidst the presence of Ishvara in his personality. Jiva's *Samsara* or suffering resided in his mind, body and intellect. Now that the presence of Ishvara is everywhere, in his mind, body, and intellect, where can *Samsara* stay in the Bhakta? He thinks, feels, acts, and wills for Ishvara's sake only and with no separate assertion of individuality. Bhakta does everything that Jiva does, like earning a degree, money, and family, but the main difference is that his center is not the separate self but an ever-connected self.

All thoughts, wills, actions, and feelings come from Bhakta's intimate relation with the Lord of the universe. Hence, he is free of *Samsara*, filled with love, peace, understanding, and truth.

Let's take a look at how Bhakta looks at the world. Bhakta looks at the world with the attitude of Bhakti. Bhakta knows that his essence is the same as the world's essence.

Due to this knowledge, he looks at the world as his family with intimacy. Bhakta thinks, "The same spirit that lives in me also lives in other human beings, animals, birds, insects, plants, planets and material objects." Bhakta acts friendly with others and the environment with this underlying thought. Bhakta looks at others in the same way siblings look at each other as connected through the same mother and father. Rather than exploiting and taking advantage of the world around him, Bhakta co-operates with the world with love for its growth. Bhakta gives gracefully to others in need without demeaning their spirit because of Bhakta's family spirit.

Neither the giver creates a superiority complex, nor the beneficiary creates an inferiority complex. Bhakta does not complain about the world as it is intimately related to him. Without Bhakti, Jiva is always in opposition, in a protecting position, or in an adjusting position with the world and even with his own family. Bhakti is a big advance in self-knowledge of a Jiva. Jiva is not born alone, but with the world in which he lives his life as soon as he opens his eyes. If one does not have the right attitude and knowledge to look at the world, his experiences will always be in conflict, resulting in anger and hostility with the world.

Whether Jiva is a philosopher, doctor, engineer, lawyer, CEO, or any other position in the world, he needs to cultivate the attitude of Bhakti to live in harmony with the world around him with which he is constantly interacting. Only the attitude of Bhakti creates a peaceful and loving environment where living beings respect, live with self-dignity, and love each other. Only an attitude of Bhakti allows one to cross a self-interested outlook which divides the world. Bhakta is a universal person. Bhakta looks at others as children of the same father independent of their race, nationality, religion, gender, age, skin, and other differences which divides man and man, and man and the environment. Bhakta has reverence for creation and himself due to an underlying common divinity. Bhakti becomes his source of inspiration and the code of conduct for his actions in the world. Bhakti turns self-becoming of a Jiva into gratitude and self-surrender. Instead of wanting to possess everything that he finds attractive in the world, a Bhakta appreciates Ishvara in those attractions. Instead of living with the attitude of enjoying sense objects, Bhakta lives with an attitude of gratitude and appreciative love for Ishvara for those sense objects. Bhakta not only sees the creation, but the creator in the creation at the same time. Rather than only benefiting from nature, he sees some additional plus value in nature. Because of his seeing of divinity in nature, he will not destroy or harm nature. Bhakti creates an auto-cooperative society of individuals. Self-knowledge backed by Bhakti solves all problems at the individual, social, national and global levels. Bhakta is a blessing to himself and the world.

Bhakti is such an important vision to achieve for a human being that Bhagavad Gita has devoted an entire chapter to it. The *Bhagavad Gita*[2] describes the characteristic marks of a Bhakta as never hating any living being, friendly, compassionate, free from the sense of possessiveness and ego, equal in pleasant and unpleasant situations, and forgiving. Because Ishvara is the center of his thought, desire, action, and relation, Bhakta gains undisturbed peace and fulfillment in the same life.

He meditates on Ishvara and does all actions for the sake of Ishvara. Because dharma, which includes the values like non-violence, truth, compassion, and selfless service, is rooted in Ishvara, commitment to dharma is commitment to Ishvara. Bhakta does not follow personal likes and dislikes, but instead is committed to the law of dharma. This commitment purifies his mind and provides relief from *Samsara*.

Bhakta's essence is Bhakti-based love or bhava. Bhakta feels himself and the world with this heart of bhava. Bhakti-based love is the purest form of love that makes a human a Godman, or a universal man. This Bhava differs from sensual attachment and is the hallmark of a devotee. Bhakti based love is the source of all saintly emotions like compassion, selfless service, parental love, and forgiveness.

Bhakta's desires, thoughts, actions, and relations are inspired by bhava alone. This makes the Bhakta a perfect instrument of the divine in the world. Bhakta's love is self-less, without expectation, impersonal, and with Ishvara as its basis. A human being always works with a motive. Bhakti makes a human being work without motive. Bhakta is able to go beyond man's limitations and work without motive, only out of love for God. This is the real miracle. Bhakta is always engaged in selfless work, because it gives Bhakta selfless love as a result. Selfless love is the touch of God. Whether Bhakta is parenting, befriending, or working, Bhakta has no other yardstick to feel the world except Bhakti based bhava. We have witnessed Buddha, Ramkrishna, Vivekananda, Gandhiji, Pandurang Shastri Athavale, and other exemplary people who spent their entire life serving mankind with Bhakti-based love without the least expectation in return.

The suffering Jiva gains peace and security after attaining the vision of Bhakti. After accepting duality, Bhakti becomes the most important vision and feeling to achieve for every human being, because it is his advancement in his self-knowledge. Bhakta is relieved from *Samsara*. His ego is diluted, or thinned out to such a level that it becomes a blessing to humanity. It's as if a poisonous snake's teeth are removed and the snake becomes harmless, decorative, and useful. Experiences of *Samsara* are removed from him through the filter of self-knowledge. He regains his original God-man stature.

Although the essence of Bhakta is the same as the essence of the world, Bhakta strongly desires to merge into its essence. It's as if a reflection of the sun in still water wants to merge with its source, the sun above. Is it possible to advance in self-knowledge and throw away even the best humanness?

Bhakta says, "I belong to Ishvara," but can an advanced Bhakta say, "I am Ishvara?" Shruti says yes. Let us explore how Ishvara, the source and sink of Jiva, sees himself.

---

1. 9.30,31
2. 12.13

Chapter Four

ISHVARA AND ANANDA

hat is Ishvara? What does his self-identity consist of? In fact, there is no other identity. It is the same Jiva who wakes up as Ishvara from the sleep of duality after self-ignorance is totally removed through self-knowledge. If Jiva sees clearly that his self is the self of all, what remains of Jivahood? Ishvara sees the world as identical to himself. His self-identity consists of existence-knowledge-ananda or *sat-chit-ananda*. He eternally exists beyond time, space, and objects. He is the self of all that exists and does not exist. He is *Sarvatma*. He is Ananda, or wholeness, and full in being because nothing more can be added or subtracted from him. His nature is permanent happiness, as opposed to fleeting happiness, in that it is not born out of any objective experience. Ishvara is a self-effulgent being, pure attribute-less *Chaitanya*, and made up of pure non-dual consciousness. He knows himself as only being of mind, body and the world. The

self of man is Ishvara. Ishvara knows him as the only identity there is. The world, mind, body, and unconscious
appear in his only identity as a city appears in a mirror. All
animated creatures and inanimate objects are but he.
There is no other and nothing else for him. It is his play-
fulness that appears as Jiva and the world. *Atma evam Idam
sarvam*. *Vedant Sutra*[1] declares *Lokvattu leela kaivalyam*. He is
the universe, and the universe is him. 'I am' is everything.
'I am' made up of pure *chit* (consciousness) and nothing is
separate from me. He sees the world as the water sees the
waves, streams and bubbles as itself playing with its own
self. Jiva and the world appear as identical to the self.
Unconscious, mind, body, and the world are all rooted in
the self. Ishvara is the world, only existence, and without
any objective qualities. *Shruti* declares 'I am' is the
Brahman that is the reality of the universe.

Jiva's progress in life is nothing but advancement in self-
knowledge. Without self-knowledge, Jiva's life is like a
dead but breathing animal. Even though it is full of activities, it is lifeless. A human being's intellect is capable of
analyzing its own experiences and reaching a final understanding. Its separate identity as Jiva is finally realized as a
cover of Ishvara, a play of duality, but cannot really cover
Ishvara after self-knowledge is gained. It is like a director
in the form of an actor playing various roles on the world-
stage.

The director, actor, other roles, stage, and spectators all
are nothing but him. *Chandogya Upanishad*[2] declares *sarvam
khalvidm brahma*.

Let us examine how this non-dual knowledge of Ishvara where, 'I am is the world,' removes the suffering of Jiva. We have already seen that suffering is an unavoidable and an unwanted pattern of experiences and memories. Jiva continuously suffers from streams of thoughts, feelings, bodily sensations, tasting, touching, perceiving, hearing, smelling, memory, and his unconscious. It is like the reflection of the sun in the sea being continuously tossed by the tides. The non-dual knowledge is the knowledge that the reflection of the sun being tossed around is in fact merely a reflection of the sun above. The sun is really unaffected or *Asang* by its nature. Vedanta guides Jiva to the solution by turning the experiencer's attention to the self instead of the objects of experience. Vedant removes suffering by removing the experiencer's identity with mind and body and recovering its true nature. By finding one's nature of self as *Asang*, one cannot be ruffled by the waves of the mind. Knowledge of one's non-dual self, Ishvara, is freedom itself. Jiva is a mind-body complex-based identity. When Jiva looks upon himself with the light of Shruti, Jiva discovers that he is Ishvara, self-effulgent being. His self-effulgence lights up the mind and body. Vedant sees human suffering as centered on his mind and body made assumed self, but not on the world or outside the Jiva. Ishvara knows that the mind, body, world and the unconscious is him, but he per se is truth, consciousness, and infinity. Ishvara's true nature is independent of the mind, body, world, and unconscious, but their being is him. Now where is the suffering? All is Ananda.

One should render ineffective impressions or *Samskara* from memory after gaining knowledge. This can be accomplished by doing vigilant contemplation regularly. *Bhagavad Gita*[3] declares that the actions or *karma* of a person who knows his identity as Ishvara are burnt down by the fire of self-knowledge. Rather than focusing on or adjusting to external and internal objective situations, Vedant makes one focus on the true nature of one's self. Vedant removes identification with not-self and ultimately resolves not-self in the self. Vedant removes threefold suffering internal to Jiva, external to Jiva, and out of control of Jiva in one stroke. By knowing that 'I am' is Ishvara, he plays freely in the world of his own making. *Mundaka Upanishad*[4] declares the world as a dualistic play of non-dual self or *atmakrida*. When one discovers his true nature is *sat-chit-ananda*, attribute-less consciousness, objective qualityless consciousness, or *nirvisheshchaitanya*, then the human experience becomes like a reflection in the mirror of consciousness and not touched by the content of reflection.

Because Ishvara is completeness/*Purna*/wholeness/Ananda/limitlessness, a major implication is that Jiva's constant and exhaustive search for happiness in an objective world ends. Jiva gets fulfilled right away, knowing happiness is his own nature. Jiva originally mistook happiness as located outside of himself and in persons and objects of the world. However, he experiences fullness as self after gaining self-knowledge. All previous excursions of Jiva for deriving complete and permanent happiness stops. Even efforts to earn good merits stop. Self-ignorance is the cause of the incorrect notion that happiness is outside and must be obtained by acquiring the desired object, person, or conditions. Jiva believes that this acquired object, person, or conditions will make him complete. Self-knowledge removes the cause and hence, all the effects such as sensual pleasures, addictions, and obsessions Jiva previously had. *Bhagavad Gita*[5] declares that such a person finds total satisfaction in the self. Such a person frees the world from the onus of making him happy. Jiva, as Ishvara, breaks out of the cycle of *Samsara* built of action/*karma* and enjoyment/*bhoga*. As an Ishvara, he is neither doer of an action nor the enjoyer. Only such an inherently happy person can bring peace and happiness to the world.

How can any sense of incompleteness exist in Ishvara where he sees himself as the immediate awareness of ananda or *Chidananda*? Such a person who has gained self-knowledge still entertains desires, but with a major change: he does not seek fulfillment through desire, but rather expresses fullness. Like the ocean is not increased or decreased from the rising and falling of the tides. Jiva is nothing but the life of becoming and wanting, while Ishvara is the playing of abundance and fullness of being.

As Ishvara, my thoughts, desires, actions, and feelings are expressions or working of myself. Hence, they cannot be limited by their specific attributes or qualities. For example, thinking at the intellect level can generate stress. But the quality of intellect generating stress can't limit me.

Because being Ishvara, intellect can't exist separate from me. Intellect is seen as a configuration or a mode of consciousness. The same is true for other faculties of the mind, like emotions, desires, and actions. As Ishvara, I am the efficient as well as the material cause of mind, body, and the world.

Since Ishvara sees the creation as identical to himself, others are seen as himself playing the role of duality. Duality is an appearance of Ishvara in the dual form of subject and object simultaneously. If I can immediately see that I in me is the same I in you, then apart from our personality differences, there is no place of hatred and ill-will for others as others are myself alone. *Ishavasya Upanishad*[6] says that such a person with his non-dual vision sees all beings in himself and sees himself in all beings. How can such a person who has a non-dual vision hate others?

Personality is an agent of doing and knowing. Personality is a cover on Ishvara in the perspective of Ishvara. The personality instrument is assumed in order to manifest a transactional dualistic world. The personality instrument is non-different from Ishvara because of being an instrument. It is Ishvara in the form of personality or ego-idea that appears as a multitude of diverse Jivas.

All the mental complexes of Jiva about separate persons or selves existing in themselves were hardening up till now. However, these mental complexes that Jiva was struggling with are now torn down and Jiva becomes liberated. Ishvara's knowledge of himself is not covered by a limited personality cover. On the other hand, Jiva is bound by personality cover and creates mental complexes. Because Jiva considers the duality of subject and object as real in itself, mental complexes are created. The enlightened Jiva naturally loves all Jivas equally because he can subtract personality differences by the love of Ishvara, who is his own self. Only such a person represents Ishvara in the human form and can unite man with man, man with the environment, man with Ishvara, and society with society due to his exclusive knowledge of non-dual unity appearing as the apparently diversified creation.

Ishvara is the *self of all*. Selfless and expectation-less love is the source of all good emotions. Compassion, service to others, forgiveness, accommodating others, non-violence, straightforwardness, truthfulness, sympathy, and friendliness are to be found in such a person. His emotions, thoughts, actions, and desires resolve into and come from the non-dual knowledge of ishvara as the self of all. Moral order, or *dharma* that brings harmony and order in the world, is natural in him. He is constantly striving to establish dharma. Conflicts and disorder are absent in his mental makeup at all. His internal and external world behaves harmoniously and orderly around the divinity of Ishvara, which is their cause.

Such a knower of non-dual only self or *Atmavid* frees himself from fear. Fear of survival, or loss of existence, due to another is born of duality. The sense of fleetingness is also centered on the notion of his knowledge of the self. Self-knowledge corrects and states that self is non-dual existence. Why would a person with non-dual knowledge fear or protect himself from others or the world? That doesn't mean that he doesn't protect himself. For example, he encounters a poisonous snake in his way. Self-knowledge makes him fearless, but he does whatever is needed to stay and enjoy in the dualistic appearance of the world. Jiva cannot enjoy the money it has earned because of the fear that it may get exhausted. Jiva's whole life is full of fear. Only Ishvara is fearless because of his non-dual knowledge of the self.

Another hallmark of *Atmavid* is that he frees himself from sorrow. *Atmavid tarati shokam* says *Chandogya Upanishad*[7].

Innumerable external and internal events can make Jiva unhappy. Ishvara cannot suffer because he is the non-dual self seeing only oneness everywhere. One can't remove sorrow without non-dual recognition of the self. A highly civilized, educated person whose character is spotless cannot remove fear and sorrow because it is built into human limitation. The only way is to aspire for the knowledge of Ishvara or self-knowledge.

Ishavasya Upanishad[8] declares that if all beings become one with the knower's self, grief and delusion are impossible because the knower sees oneness everywhere. This vision is the perfect cure for all mental distortions such as loneliness. One who sees oneness everywhere is never alone in the forest without any company, while an ignorant man feels lonely in the midst of the crowds of friends.

A person who knows himself to be the self of all does not remain as a person, but becomes God on earth and a source of inspiration for the world. He rises above all its human limitations and is fulfilled (*kruta krutya*) as all deeds needed to be done are done. Nothing is left to be done for him. This special and final fulfilment comes to a human being as a result of achieving the highest possible achievement in human life. He has perfected human life. What effort is left for him? He is looked upon as a spiritual role model for the others. In his presence, the man starts seeing order and purpose of human life rather than chaos and disorder. Every Jiva is busy with a myriad of different activities, ultimately for Ananda. A Jiva with self-knowledge personifies Ananda. He naturally attracts people irrespective of their age, race, nationalism, color, and gender because he fulfills the fundamental need for all humans striving for perfection. Why am I here? What I am supposed to be doing? Who am I? Where am I going? Where did I come from? What is my relation to Ishvara and the world? What is the best thing I can do, know, or achieve? All these questions, which are relevant to discriminative individuals and fundamental to human existence, are answered in the presence of the knower of the self.

We keep saying that Ishvara experiences the world as himself. What is this self of all? Let us only briefly touch this topic as the self can't be defined. Self is the culmination of self-knowledge. The self is the non-relational, immediate awareness of I that is the subjectless and

objectless experience or knowledge: *Nitya aparokshanubhuti.*
The world, body, mind, and unconscious, or *idam*, is not
seen or experienced through mind or any other medium
except identical to oneself as an expression or the play of
the self as *sat-chitananda*. The *Bhagavad Gita*[9] declares that
the tree of *Samsara*, or the world, body, mind, and unconscious, is upside down with its roots pointing upward as
the conscious self of man. Ishvara is the self that resolves
all manifestations of the tree and liberates man from the
puzzle of experiences derived from the world, mind, body,
and even unconscious. Thus, Ishvara is not only the
resolver of his own creation but also the maintainer, while
we are transacting with the experience of the world.
Ishvara, the self of all, solves the issue of *Idam*, or the issue
that the world, mind, body, and unconscious exist independently with their own existence and outside the self.

Ishvara is the maker and the material cause of the *Idam*.
The existence of an object is the existence of the self
alone.

Self is not an abstract notion, but instead is the non-dual
subject, the objectless reality of experience, and in other
words, the root experience. This does not mean that self is
one experience amongst innumerable experiences which
must be found. Self is the root of experience, *Lokan*, or
what is experienced.

When all superimpositions or assumed notions of the self
are removed by perfect self-knowledge, the bare self of a
human being, pure consciousness, *chaitanyam* Ishvara, the

self of all, or the root of all experiences is recovered. After rising to this non-dual vision of the self, our experience is no more conditioned by or filtered by the dualistic notion of the self. Everything is experienced as self or "I am" like a person recognizes himself in front of a mirror. This recognition of "I am is all this" or *aham idam sarvam asmi* is the non-dual vision of Ishvara is revealed by *Shurti* to a human being. Attribute-less self, or "I am" is the essence of being of the universe. Knowing you are the essence of the universe makes you Ishvara.

Generally, we see ourselves as this limited personality; I am knower, doer, enjoyer, hearer, smeller, eater, feeler, perceiver, thinker, and many other notions which are all derived from "I am this or that". All of these notions are variable and changing based on the condition or *Upadhi* "I" takes.

This "variable I" is "vulnerable I" and "the affected and hurtful I", which gathers guilt, hurt, and emotional scars or impressions on the human being's unconscious mind. Objects of the world persecute him at every moment. One has to face undesirable and unexpected conditions every day.

This makes the human-being subject to *Samsara*. When Ishvara's vision is attained, what really happens is that the ego notion of the self, as a limited personality, or subtle body, is falsified. The importance of self-knowledge is the highest knowledge in a human being's life because without knowing the real nature of self or essence of man, these notional superimpositions on the self as "variable I" can never ever go away. Self-ignorance is the cause of these superimpositions on the self and hence requires correction through clear knowledge of the self. After correction, every object's existence and happiness is seen as belonging to the self and made up of pure consciousness or *Chaitanya*. Only then will objects lose their binding power, and only then will one become realized with the vision of Ishvara as the self of all. This is termed as liberation in life. *Shruti* calls such a Jiva *Jivan-mukta*, or liberated while alive.

Such a *Jivan-mukta* person becomes carefree about his earnings for his own living and loves all living beings. Jivanmukta's thoughts, desires, and actions transform from personal to universal where the purpose becomes to do good to all or lok-sangrah. *Jivan-mukta* is a real friend of humanity. *Jivan-mukta* works for all and not for a particular race, color, country, age, gender, or cast. Such a liberated individual constantly works for the upliftment of human beings. Such a liberated individual constantly works to make human beings aware of their spiritual and divine nature. Just like a blind man is unaware of the surrounding treasure that he is placed with, a human being is ignorant about its divine potential. *Jivan-mukta* removes suffering by showing that the self of an individual is Ishvara, *asamsari,* or free from suffering. *Jivanmukta* connects the human being to its peaceful divine essence and constantly works to bring out that divinity in the human being. Vivekananda once said that, "Alas! If you know yourself, you are the *Paramata* or supreme self, I feel like I am condemning Ishvara when I call you a human being." *Jivan-mukta's* desires are expressions of fullness. His thoughts remove self-ignorance and his actions bring out total satisfaction in oneself. *Jivan-mukta's* life, deeds, desires, and thoughts reveal that the highest destination for a human being is to recognize its divine self as Ishvara and to remove self-ignorance by obtaining self-knowledge. *Jivan-mukta's* life shows that everything or *idam* is not inside or outside Ishvara, but is Ishvara, which is the recognition of one's own essential, intimate, ever present, and innermost attribute-less self.

Jivanmukta joins man to Ishvara, man to man, man to animals, man to plants, and man to the environment. *Jivanmukta* advocates spiritual values and not materialism. *Jivanmukta's* life shows the ladder for a human being's progress from deriving pleasure from objects or *Vishayananda*, to emotional happiness or *Bhavananda*, to intellectual happiness or *Vidyananda*, and finally to happiness or *Ananda* itself as self.

---

1. 2.1.33
2. 3.14.1
3. 4.37
4. 3.1.4
5. 2.55
6. 6
7. 7.1.3
8. 7
9. 15.1

Chapter Five

RECOGNITION OF THE SAME SELF

The vision of sameness develops by recognizing that one's self is the same self of all beings. This is the biggest implication of the knowledge of Ishvara. The most natural way of living after realizing self as Ishvara is loving all beings and oneself because of this vision of the identity of self in all beings or *Samatva Darshna*. This is the liberating vision because it frees a human being from uncomfortable feelings that he cannot face. Unable to face these feelings, suffering is created. This recognition of the same self in all beings turns a human being into a sage or seer. A person is a sage or seer not due to having a beard, degree, particular skin color, nationality, or gender, but because he beholds this profound vision of equality in all beings and lives according to that vision. Because the vision is founded on the self-same reality of beings, it creates the best destiny for a human being and the world. One can free oneself by the liberating vision of recognizing the same self every-where. This is the vision of peace, fulfilment, and happiness.

Bhagavad Gita[1] declares that a human being hurts himself by himself when ignoring this vision that is a result of self-knowledge. Let us see how a human being creates its own suffering in a nutshell. In other words, let us see how a human being ignores self-knowledge. While living life, a human being develops uncomfortable feelings for other beings and himself. Examples of uncomfortable feelings are anger, dislike, hate, jealousy, envy, guilt, hurt, and contempt. These feelings are uncomfortable because they create conflict in himself and his intellect cannot find a solution to handle them. As a result, these feelings need to be pushed into the unconscious. These unsolved conflicts in the unconscious become hardened over time and make the knot of suffering. For example, I dislike and hate a person due to his awkward personality traits, which are totally different from mine. There is practically no way to solve this conflict. Even though I try to either shun him away from me or avoid him altogether, his mere remem-brance is enough to resurface the uncomfortable feelings in me. Moreover, I cannot avoid all circumstances to refrain from him. For example, he is a colleague or closely related. Next time when I will encounter him, I will see him immediately with the already built complex which invokes and deepens ill feelings. Over time, a human being fills up his unconscious with these uncomfortable feelings.

The unconscious becomes heavier and heavier, as time goes on because situations keep recreating more complexes and more deeply rooted complexes.

The problem of a heavy unconscious is like a trash bag getting filled up, but with no dumpster to empty it. The heavier the unconscious becomes with uncomfortable feelings, the more suffering such a person experiences. The signs of such a personality are remaining angry, hateful, and complaining. Even a light situation evokes a heavy response from such a person. Such a person is happy for a moment, but then suddenly becomes sad because of memories from the unconscious of some uncomfortable feelings. Such a person looks at other persons and himself with prejudices, through the built-in complexes, and will not give any chance to improve those prejudices. It is like a dog with his tongue sticking out and barking constantly at whoever he encounters. A human being suffers because of the pressure from its unconscious.

Be careful. Ill-feelings, thoughts, wishes, and actions are mostly gathered towards whoever you are interacting most with. It may be towards your closest family member like your son, wife, daughter, husband, father, mother, brother, sister, colleague, supervisor, close friend, or a close relative like an uncle or aunt. For example, I do not care how others' son behaves, but if my son or daughter behaves repetitively against what I like, there is a possibility of creating an unhealthy complex in the mind about my intimate ones.

In order to remove uncomfortable feelings for others and yourself, understand and recognize clearly that the essential self in you is the same self that dwells in all beings, before the essential self in you becomes personality or qualified with mind and body adjuncts. Only the vision based on the truth can take a human being to its final goal of liberation from unwanted mutations or *Samsara*. As a person with a mind, body adjuncts, one cannot be the same as others. A wooden chair and wooden table look different in name and form. If divested of name and form, the wood, or in other words the essential self, is recognized as the same in both. Although personality differs from a being to a being due to mind and body differences, their essential, innermost and bare self, which is *Atma* or self-evident Ishvara, is identical in all beings. I am the non-dual self before any personality adjuncts. After gaining this self-knowledge, I cannot have contempt, hate, dislike, disdain, anger, or other ill feelings, thoughts, wishes, and actions for myself or others.

Let us create the most beneficial contemplation or *nididhyasana* for a human being based on this non-dual vision of Ishvara, the self of all. The purpose of this contemplation is to remove all uncomfortable feelings distorting and troubling human beings. Let us create a simple contemplation based on this vision, which can empty out the heavy unconscious of a human being and can break unwanted complexes against the non-dual vision of the self. This contemplation is of the highest value and worth, deserves to spend our time as it removes ill-feelings towards others and yourself. This contemplation is liberating and has the highest value because it sees the dark-complexes of a human being using the light of the non-dual truth.

When you are meditating, bring the being to the attention in your mind to whom you hate, contempt, are angry at, or have bad feelings towards. That being will come forward from your unconscious. Memories associated with that being will surface with conditions causing the complexes. See that the causes of creating complexes in the first place lie in the attributes, qualities, or character traits differences between me and that person. Then apply this non-dual vision of the self. Shift ill feelings towards attributes, qualities, and not towards the essential self, because the essential self is identical as me, before it becomes personality. That is, focus on the essentiality of a person subtracting its attributes of behavior, actions, thoughts, wishes, and traits. Know, and see clearly that the essential self, *satchitananda* is the same in me and that being. That means if I hate you means I hate myself and same for other ill feelings. The sting of ill-feeling will disappear in time because there is no basis for their support, sustenance, or survival. Remember, this contemplation is a healing or curing of all our ill-feeling about ourselves and others based on non-dual vision. The peaceful nature of self will manifest, and the unconscious will be released from the pressure of these impressions of uncomfortable feelings. A light unconscious is the real freedom as one can enjoy the world as it is without the filter of prejudices. It is the tiny ego-self that gathers unwanted complexes, and that is replaced here by this contemplation practice with the essential shared self of all beings, *satchitananda*. Not only can this contemplation destroy ill impressions, but due to the strength of contemplation, non-dual vision will stabilize and will stop the formation of new complexes even if unexpected behaviors, situations, people, or traits are encountered.

Make sure that no beings become the target of our anger, hatred, contempt, or ill-feelings. Using this contemplation or vision of sameness of Ishvara in all, we can purify our unconscious, reform our conscious mind, and bring peace and happiness to ourselves. Only a peaceful person can distribute peace to the environment and nobody else. This is the biggest service to mankind and one self. Stabilize in the *advait* or non-dual vision and contemplation and then immerse in thoughts, desires, and various activities of the world. This is the absolute best for all human beings as it takes one to the highest destiny reserved for human beings called liberation, joy, peace, and immortality.

The vision based on Ishvara is the most beneficial to a human being because it takes one to the highest destiny or potential. One learns to accept himself, and others based on the love of Ishvara. On the other hand, it does not mean that a sage lives a passive life of acceptance.

A sage has always been established in the shared reality of beings. Hence, he is internally free from complexes and intimate with every human being. A sage guides and inspires humanity through this vision to humanity's highest destiny by suggesting, implementing improvements, activities, and programs leading to this vision, and establishes this vision in a human being. By the recognition of the same self everywhere and in all beings or *Samatva Darshan*, a person can overcome his shortcomings and become a blessing to himself and the world.

---

1. 13.28

Chapter Six

STORY OF THE TENTH MAN

Ten boys were studying at their Guru's home. Once, the boys wanted to visit their families in the village across the river. The guru designated the eldest boy as a leader to oversee the group. The boys approached the river and began to swim. While swimming, the boys happened to be separated because of the river's strong currents. All reached the other bank of the river dripping wet. The leader found them, gathered them, and made them line up one-by-one in order to properly count if anybody had drowned or not reached yet. He started counting one, two,....., nine. The leader boy counted that only nine boys were present and concluded that the tenth boy was missing. The leader panicked. What would he tell his teacher? What would he tell the family of the drowned boy? He was helplessly screaming, recounting, and thinking about the drowned boy.

A wise old man was sitting nearby and watching the way the event unfolded. He approached the leader, consoled him, and said that he could help find the missing body. He and the leader asked the boys to line up again. The leader started counting again one, two…, nine. The leader was in despair and was weeping that there were still only nine. The wise man turned to the leader and said, "You are the missing tenth man." Suddenly and immediately, the leader realized his mistake and elated, "I am the tenth man." The leader had mistakenly understood that one boy had drowned and had caused pain and despair to everyone. He had overlooked and forgotten himself while counting!

This is a simple story, but has profound implications. Let us see how it relates to us and what we can get from it. In the story, the leader, the tenth man, has done everything he could do, subtracting himself, which caused all kinds of pain and despair. The story ends happily once the mistake of not counting himself was corrected. Similarly, we pass life in gathering all kinds of experiences that we desire. They are always followed by pain, fleeting pleasure, and seeking, which keeps us in *Samsara*. We live in experiences, but never develop the tendency to discriminate and learn from the data of experiences. Until now, we have clearly seen that a human being's experience, which consists of thoughts, desires, emotions, actions, and perceptions, all have a single root out of which they come, sink, and are being maintained. That root is how one perceives himself or self-knowledge. According to one's self-knowledge, one's experiences will follow.

The tenth man in the story ignored the most basic and precious thing in life: the self. Similarly, we keep busy in gathering education, possessions, relationships, entertainment, money, and health, but do not pay attention to our own self. Our notions about ourselves are ambiguous, mistaken, beliefs, and guesses. That turns our experiences into *Samsara*.

A person tries to complete himself endlessly, but will never be able to find fullness, happiness, peace, and immortality because something very basic is not considered in the equation. That is the self as it is. "I am" is known to us, but "what I am" is not understood. Nothing in the objective kingdom can complete us subtracting the knowledge of oneself because the self is the root of all beings. We keep ourselves busy with eating, drinking, thinking of various objects, relating, sightseeing, feeling different emotions, entertaining and other activities. Continuously dwelling on the experiences and thinking that some experience will complete us one day is the same problem as of the tenth man of counting again and again. We repeat or count again and enhance experiences to fulfill ourselves. Instead, one must generate the knowledge of the self with the help of Vedant. The *Bhagavad Gita*[1] declares that one should elevate oneself through one's mind. In other words, one should study and understand one's own experience in the light of *Shruti* to develop self-knowledge. If one does not seek self-knowledge, then that same mind can act as its own enemy, making one lost like the tenth man.

Vedant is an experiential analysis of human experiences. Vedant shows us our own face, or real nature of a human being. Self-knowledge needs to travel with the help of Vedant or *Shruti* or guru of Vedant from Jiva to Bhakta and from Bhakta to Ishvara for liberation from *Samsara*. Vedant is a source of knowledge, like a wise old man in the story who guides human beings towards his ultimate destination.

One may argue that it is really tedious to learn Vedant and then apply or verify that learning in the midst of all that is going on in life. First, it should be of greatest desire to learn about oneself because it is human beings first need as previously discussed. Second, learning about oneself is never tedious because the self is *Ananda* or happiness. Because the nature of self is always available and present, one does not need to verify its learning later like we need to do in learning other relative knowledge or *Apara Vidya*. What we are talking about here is the knowledge about oneself or *Para Vidya*, and learning about oneself is always immediately learned.

Self-knowledge is the immediate learning because the self is the one who is learning and available always to verify at the same time. Here on the topic of self-knowledge, the subject and object of learning is the same and hence it is immediately learned. Just like the tenth man immediately learned and rejoiced when told that he was the tenth man, self-knowledge is immediately learned. Self-knowledge is never abstract learning of ideas and wishful thinking, but concrete immediate experience of oneself because self or

Atman is the nature of immediate awareness. If a person uses his intellect in the endeavor of acquiring self-knowledge, he immediately fulfills himself, as there is nothing left to be done. Such a person is called intellectually rich in the *Bhagavad Gita*[2].

The other mistaken notion about self-knowledge is that I can learn it myself because I know myself. Well, that is exactly the problem. What we know about oneself is faulty and erroneous. The whole problem of *Samsara* can be reduced to the superimposition of not-self upon the self. *Samsara* is ultimately rooted in *avidya* or self-ignorance. Like the tenth man was in error of always subtracting himself, one can't arrive at the solution unless pointed out by a source of knowledge present at the situation. The one who is in the midst of experiences, its own identity, is veiled by self-ignorance. A human being can learn about other than himself with his eyes, ears, mind, and intellect. However, there is no instrument to learn about oneself because the self is not an object that one can learn with a microscope. That is why Vedant, *Shruti,* or guru's help is required for developing self-knowledge. Vedant guides us in correcting wrong notions that we entertain about the self. Vedant uproots self-ignorance until we arrive at the self-knowledge or real nature of the self as the self of all, Ishvara.

Self is an immediate awareness, adjunctless consciousness, or *Nirupadhik Chaitanya*. The nature of self makes self-knowledge easy and more useful to learn than anything else. *Bhagavad Gita*[3] declares that knowledge centered on the self must always be pursued with commitment and with the understanding that it leads to liberation and immortality; while opposing values and priorities in life other than self-knowledge is ignorance. Only knowledge that makes us permanently happy and secure is self-knowledge. After all, happiness and security is the prime purpose behind every human pursuit. If I pursue professional knowledge that is fine, but it can't make me happy and secure. The question is, which knowledge makes me a real human by invoking human values? Which knowledge leads me to Ishvara, which is complete fulfillment and immortality in the present life itself?

The moral of the tenth man story is that a human being needs to consciously decide the significance of self-knowledge and commit to the effort of ultimate welfare or *Moksha*.

---

1. 6.6
2. 15.20
3. 13.11

Chapter Seven

ENTERING SELF-KNOWLEDGE

*E*ntering self-knowledge requires having the maturity of mind to be able to gain entry into self-knowledge. Self-knowledge becomes important only after certain understanding comes to a human mind. This understanding is like a key to open the door to the Vedant. Without this understanding, man still lives, but cannot unlock the mystery of human life.

As a human being, we dwell into objective experiences from birth till death. We act tirelessly to make ourselves happy and in order to better experience. The goal of our actions is always eternal happiness and security. We are always working for a better experience, which proves that the goal of our actions is not reached. As soon as we are born, we grow, educate ourselves, get a good job and insurance, have a family and do some charity work. We get all these things, but we still have to keep working to get a better and better experience. In this process of continuous action for getting better and better, we age, but the goal appears at a distance. Mature human beings sit back and look at all experiences and fruits of actions objectively rather than continuously dwelling on individual experiences. They come to the conclusion that they do not want ephemeral happiness and security. They realize that after so much hard labor until now, they only got fleeting happiness and security. One questions whether any form of action can bring eternal happiness? As actions itself are temporary, how can it bring lasting results? Once the fruit of actions perish, I go back to a stage of an eternal seeker. For example, I earned so much money and fame during some period, but it perished after some time and now I remain the same seeker as I was before I earned that money and fame. All objective experiences or *lokan* are the fruits of my actions that will one day perish, and I will become a miserable seeker again. *Mundaka Upanishad*[1] says the created cannot produce uncreated or *Nasty Akrath Kritena*. The unproduced cannot be produced by any amount of action.

The temporary nature of action and its fruits cannot bring everlasting results. One becomes dispassionate after gaining this understanding that all that action can do is provide me with some comforts for a while. While the fruits of my actions can last for a few number of years, it is still going to end after which I will go back to square one from where I started. With this dispassionate mind, one turns in the direction of self-knowledge in search of the eternal and approaches a guru or *Shruti*. The eternal self can only be discovered or unveiled through self-knowledge. This is where one enters into the doors of the Vedant asking for the knowledge of the self that is eternally happy, secure, uncreated, and non-dual.

Buddhi or human intellect is equipped with the ability to cognize the real nature of things. We need to use this ability of the human mind to aim or turn towards the real nature of the self. This ability of buddhi is used in Vedant to inquire about the real nature of self.

Another ability of the mind is to meditate without aiming at the real nature of self. This ability is a mental action without the goal of cognizing the real nature of a thing. One example is a meditation on God and repeatedly thinking that I am God or like a God. In this case, I already know that I am such-and-such and I am trying to superimpose God on me. This can help only a dispersed mind to become one pointed and gathered, but not useful at a later stage where the real nature of the self needs to be discovered.

It should be clear to the aspirant that we are not looking for some, yet to come, objective experience of the mind, but the goal is to turn to the self which is manifesting as all objective experiences, *Anubhuti Svarupa*.

We established above that maturity in the form of understanding of the mind, determines the entry into the self-knowledge. Let us explore one by one some useful means of self-knowledge.

---

1. 1.2.12

Part Two

MEANS OF SELF-KNOWLEDGE

Chapter Eight

DISCRIMINATING REAL FROM UNREAL

*E*very human being needs to discover himself as *satchitananda* or Ishvara. A human being is equipped with an intellect or *buddhi*. The power of thinking and discrimination needs to be developed in order to arrive at what 'I am' really is. Since the power of knowledge is concerned with the real nature of things, it can discriminate reality or 'what is' from falsehood or 'what is not'. *Buddhi* can dive into the darkness and can arrive at a conclusion about the reality of things.

Ignorance and doubt here are about a human being's self. Doubt is in the *buddhi* of a human being in the form of whether the self is complete or incomplete, whether I am limited or unlimited, mortal or immortal, and happy or unhappy. Here, doubt is because of non-discrimination. Here, ignorance is self-ignorance and doubt is self-doubt. The only way to correct this is to develop discrimination about the reality of self and not-self. Discerning self from not-self or *Atma-anatma Viveka* is the precursor to self-knowledge. *Atma-anatma viveka* is discerning what stays or *Nitya* and what is fleeting or *Anitya* in a human being's experience.

Let us take a story of two men who travelled through a forest to get to their village at night. One man saw a ghost in the forest. He trembled, sweated, screamed, and told his friend to run. The second man was wise and turned on a flashlight. He pointed the flashlight in the direction of the ghost. He smiled. He consoled his friend that it was a tree and not a ghost. In the story, the wise man with a flashlight is like a person who has developed his power of discrimination in the direction of real and unreal, self and not-self. It is the discriminative knowledge that weeds out fleetingness or unreality from the reality. Most people, like the man in the story, use discrimination for everything other than self, keep doubting, and remain in ignorance about Ishvara, the self, and the world. They keep themselves as *samasari* or an afflicted person and cannot move an inch in terms of self-knowledge. Notions about oneself can change as life goes on, but whether it is correct is unknown. A clear vision is not created about the self. One needs to analyze their experiences in the light of Vedant or *Shruti* and develop the power of discrimination to be able to distinguish self from not-self and its *Svarup* or real nature.

The sweating, screaming and fearing state of a man, while experiencing the world, is like travelling in the forest without a flashlight even though one has been endowed with intellect. The *Bhagavad Gita*[1] says to a man to cut asunder self-doubt and self-ignorance by developing thinking and discrimination about self and not-self.

If my buddhi concludes that I am bound by pain and pleasure, then, however I try to avoid pain, I will always be affected. Even pleasure turns into pain. Instead, if I discern self from not-self from my own experiences and realize that self is not affected by pain and pleasure, because the self is not the doer, then even in the midst of pain and pleasure I will remain unaffected. If I know that I am immortal, undying, imperishable, or *Amrut Svarup*, how can death, disease, and gray hair affect me? If I know that I am peaceful by nature, then any agitations in mind or body cannot shake me up. If I know that I am the non-dual, whole self, then differences in mind, body, and personality between you and me will not lessen my love for you. If I know that I am the source of happiness, then any object or person cannot allure me. If I know that I am knowledge itself or *Chit Svarup*, then what other knowledge do I seek? *Shvetashvatara Upanishad*[2] declares that man's sorrow comes to an end without knowing the self only if he can roll up the sky. In other words, it is impossible to end the sorrow and misery of a human being without acquiring the knowledge of the self.

Remember, this is not an abstract knowledge that I am trying to achieve. It is about the most intimate, only concrete, or real and stable self of mine. Self-discrimination leads to the essence of our being by removing the mixed in non-essential parts of our experience. Knowledge derived out of discrimination based on one's own experiences will be final and will not diminish in any case. Removed doubt and ignorance through discrimination will never come back. All objective experiences come and go away, even if it is a trance or *samadhi* experience. Still, the self's knowledge, derived from discrimination, does not go away because it is about the eternal self. Discrimination and inquiry that one can do about the self and not-self is the boat that carries one to the other shore of *Samsara*.

---

1. 4.42
2. 6.20

Chapter Nine

INQUIRING INTO THE SELF

S elf-inquiry, or *Atma Vichar,* is the means to produce self-knowledge. Once one finds that one's inherent troubles, fear, seeking, and sorrow are all due to not knowing oneself, commitment and love for self-inquiry becomes obvious. Self-inquiry is the most precious and joyous effort one can do in one's life. Self-inquiry is necessary as we take ourselves to be granted as 'I am like this or that' and stop inquiring about the self in the light of Vedant. Our whole life is spent in the effort of finding happiness, peace, and immortality in not-self or objects and never in looking in the direction of self for the same. We become exhausted and frustrated, take ourselves as limited, subject to sorrow, and always seeking means as a *samsari.* Once we have enough discrimination from experience, we start asking about the real nature of ourselves. Once the desire for self-knowledge rises after discriminating between ephemeral and eternal, the guru of non-dual teachings, Vedant, is needed. Self-inquiry means asking the question 'who am I,' 'what am I,' or 'what is the real nature to whom reference is done as I.' Self-inquiry is an inquiry and discrimination of Vedant's great saying or *Vedant Vakya Vichar* like 'Thou art that' or *Tatvamasi*.

Shravanam, i.e., listening from a qualified teacher of non-dual teaching of Vedant is the first step of self-inquiry. Through constantly referring to the texts of the *Shruti*, lectures from a guru, and through discussions with similarly oriented family and friends, one tries to understand self as an experiential understanding like a tenth man. This step needs to be continued until one comes to a clear conclusion about the real nature of self as described in Vedant.

Vedant or *Shruti* teaches different methods to produce self-knowledge. These methods are an analysis of a human being's experience. For example, *Mandukya Upanishad* deals with discrimination of three states of our experience or *Avastha Tray Viveka*, *Taittiriya Upanishad* deals with discrimination of five sheaths or *Pancha Kosha Viveka*, and *Chandogya Upanishad* deals with discrimination of cause and effect or *Karya Karan Viveka*. *Bhagavad Gita* and *Upanishads* most commonly deal with discrimination between seer and seen or *Drk Drysa Viveka*.

These methods and others are very important, unfailing methods that systematically take a seeker to the sought. These methods are needed in all steps of self-inquiry.

Pondering or reflecting about the self to remove doubts about the other views of the self, or *Manan,* and bringing out the clarity of the self as described in the Shruti, is the second step of self-inquiry. For example, one can ponder for some time after reading a book or listening to a lecture on non-dual teaching. This step is very important because it refutes all opposing views of the self after seeing the errors. This step is needed until all opposing views are refuted and we can settle down to a conclusion about non-dual existence, knowledge, and Ananda nature of the self.

Meditating on the self, or *Nididhyasana,* is the final step in the self-inquiry. The purpose of this step is twofold. First, is to reverse the mind and clearly see the cognitive process, or mind that a human being is. One needs to clearly see that the mind or cognitive process starts, sinks and is being maintained in and as the self. In other words, the self is the essence of mind. It allows one to face the self, to abide as the self, or to meditate on the attribute-less self. The second purpose of meditation is to live as implied by the new discovery of the real nature of self. In other words, re-align our thoughts, feelings, and desires to match the non-dual self. We need to replace our old impressions that are opposing new knowledge like an old street dog does not allow a new stranger dog to take over the street.

A lost cub of a lioness grew up in a flock of sheep. The cub was bleating as sheep bleat and was eating grass like a sheep. The cub also ran when some wild animal attacked the flock. Over time, the cub became a young lion eating the grass. One day, a wild lion saw the grass eating lion and was surprised. The wild lion attacked the flock and took the young lion near a pond. He asked the young lion to stop bleating and to look at the reflection in the pond. The young lion looked at his reflection and bleated. Then, the wild lion asked if he could find any difference between the two lions. The young lion compared his reflection with the wild lion's reflection and rejoiced, "I am the same as you!" The wild lion roared and asked the young lion to roar like him. The young lion roared.

The story depicted above shows the importance of self-inquiry in order to arrive at the real nature of self with the guidance of Vedant or a qualified guru. A human being always grows up as samsari, an afflicted person, tossed between pain and pleasure, just as the cub grew up as bleating sheep.

However, the life of a human being is about growth in self-knowledge until he realizes he is *Asamsari*, or the Ananda nature of self. Truly living a human life is growing the desire for liberation or truth, discriminating between eternal and ephemeral, being dispassionate or attributing correct value to things, calming mind and body, drawing lines of satisfaction for possessions like wealth, health, fame, power, having faith, and cultivating forbearance leading to self-inquiry. Possession of these virtues turns one into a seeker of reality. *Bhagavad Gita*[1] advocates that such a seeker should practice self-inquiry regularly, keeping in mind that the fruit of self-knowledge is liberation. Such a seeker practicing self-inquiry regularly would obtain the result of liberation or *Moksha* and become the sought.

Meditation and concentration play a significant role in self-inquiry and hence in acquiring self-knowledge. Let us see how meditation, concentration, and other means can support self-inquiry leading to self-knowledge.

---

1. 13.11

Chapter Ten

TURNING AROUND THE MIND

urning around the mind is meditation. Paying attention to the self is meditation. To gain self-knowledge, turning around the mind from its natural direction towards objects is a must. One must reverse the mind and senses from the objects to the source of mind. *Katha Upanishad*[1] says that the reversal of mind is possible, but this direction of mind towards the self is not known or practiced by a person until one desires immortality and freedom. Turning around the mind resolves the mind into the self. Self is the source, sink, and pervader of the mind even while it is functioning. The aspirant first needs to gather the mind from various activities such as sensing, feeling, thinking, perceiving, testing, smelling, touching, and hearing, and then must be made aware of its own source until it resolves into self or *Atman*.

Generally, the mind is always running outward towards objects and so the self is veiled. As soon as a person wakes up, he starts rushing for various activities oriented towards objects. This is a natural direction of a human being's mind because it is constituted to seek out various objects of desire. At night, a person's mind tires of these sense activities and wants to sleep. The mind gets tired of constantly attending to the object of experiences. Although objects of experiences are changing during a lifetime, the mind's direction and pull towards objects of desire is always the same. It's as if a businessman leases his shop, but barely makes money to pay for the lease. The businessman keeps earning money, but gives it all for rent and never makes a profit. The life of a human being is a blind run towards various objects of desire in which it never gets peace, immortality and permanent happiness that it seeks.

A new direction of turning the mind and paying attention to the self is necessary and must condition for a human being's ultimate destiny. Generally, people do some meditation to get some rest and gather up enough energy to run around for a day. This is not meditation's real benefit and goal. Meditation is an important habit for a human being to break forth the cycle of *Samsara* and suffering by seeing the self, or one's own true being, Ishvara. Meditation, if done properly as guided by Vedant, resolves the mind into the self and develops self-knowledge.

The *Bhagavad Gita*[2] declares that the thirst for various objects of fleeting enjoyments, or *Trishna*, cannot go away until one sees the immortal and *Ananda* nature of the self. The desire for fleeting happiness stays until one sees the self as the source of eternal happiness. Turning around the mind towards self and resolving the mind into the self is like changing the flow of a river in the reverse direction. Meditation is preceded by concentration of mind which gathers up the mind from its various pursuits. The restless nature of the mind goes away once it tastes the peaceful, or *Shanta* nature of the self and then it moves around undisturbed into the various objects. Meditation is staying as oneself, as self-refulgent being or *Chaitanya Atma* – as one really is. Meditation breaks the natural habit of mind to constantly run after objects and develops self-knowledge. The desire for various objects of enjoyment, or *Kama*, is reduced and is nullified by seeing *Ananda* atman. Without the counter habit of meditation, how can a person break forth the natural habit of rushing for various objective experiences, or *lokan*? Meditation opens up a brand-new direction for a meditator which was previously unknown, towards an objectless direction to the source of mind.

Meditation thus allows the possibility to reveal the true nature of a human being as Ishvara, which was denied by self-ignorance or *Avidya*. Generally, a human being is bound by the body and mind and is always repeating some activities in mind or body level. Meditation helps a person to break the law of *karma* and allows him to stay as the self, where the law of *karma* does not operate. Meditation resolves objects into the self and thus reveals the self as creator, sustainer, and material of all objects, the cause of the world, or Ishvara. When the self wants to light up the objective experiences, it creates attention or orientation towards the objective direction. After that, the self veils and the mind is active. Meditation makes a person rise above the mind into its source, that is the self as it is.

The mind is an expression of the self-evident self. Not knowing the self, mind behaves as bondage. While knowing the self, the mind becomes an expression of the freedom of self. Not understanding the identity of mind creates suffering of a human being. By realizing self or *SatChitAnanda* as the essence of mind and by developing self-knowledge, one can free oneself from the bondage of *Samsara*. A human being is an identity composed of mind and body. When a human being realizes its true self, or identity, is a conscious being free of mind, free of the body, and instead the cause of mind and body, then it becomes free while living, or a *Jivanmukta*.

Meditation, or paying attention to the self, plays a very key role in revealing the true nature of the self of a human being. To reverse the natural activities of the mind from its objects towards the self is a big task and needs to be preceded by first gathering up the mind from its various objective activities. One should strongly seek permanent happiness, look for immortality, and know that until now, the direction in which one was seeking happiness can only give fleeting happiness but never permanent happiness. Discriminating thus, one creates dispassion for an objective direction towards objects and is able to turn one's mind around. *The Bhagavad Gita*³ declares that practice and dispassion make meditation successful.

Meditation is aligning to the self or *Brahmacharya*. The practice of meditation daily is a very important practice of *Brahmacharya*. It allows one to re-align, abide, or stay as self. Gradually, restlessness of mind is suffused with the peaceful and happy nature of the non-dual self. Even while wandering in the midst of objects, the mind keeps its nature of peace and happiness, which is the real freedom. Meditation reveals the invariable, and constant nature of self in the midst of changing and variable sense activities. The mind's projecting power comes under the control of the meditator by knowing the self appears as the mind. The chase for various sense objects ceases or quietens due to meditation leading to the realization of the self. All objects of the desires are obtained at once upon knowing the self says *Taittiriya Upanishad*⁴.

---

1. 2.1.1
2. 2.59
3. 6.35
4. 2.1.1

Chapter Eleven

CONCENTRATING THE MIND

*M*editation is preceded by concentration of mind. Naturally, the raw mind rushes in all directions towards different topics and subjects. To make the mind able to dwell upon a single subject for some time is a necessary step. Mind by nature is a variable stream of thoughts, emotions, sensations and perceptions of taste, hear, touch, see, and smell. Concentration is not the effort to stop the mind's flow because the mind is the flow. Instead, concentration is withdrawing the mind from various different directions and channelizing it to a chosen topic or subject and letting it flow around the same common subject or topic for some time. The mind should not be allowed to jump all over through the diverse channels of the mind. Concentration of the mind, or *Chit Ekagrata*, results in a stable and mature mind ready for meditation.

As the mind is totally receptive, it is recommended that it should be focused on Ishvara, a chosen deity, or divine incarnation. The *Bhagavad Gita*[1] says to put one's mind in Ishvara with qualities, or *Shagun Brahma*. The mind sees things in terms of its qualities. In order to make a fickle and dispersed mind gathered and stable, the chosen center of focus of the mind must have the best qualities, which is ultimately God, a deity, Ishta Devata, or incarnations of God such as Krishna, Rama, Jesus, or Buddha. Because the mind is receptive, its thoughts, sensations, emotions, and perceptions start flowing around Ishvara with qualities it can think, feel, and perceive. One can sing devotional songs or hymns to prepare the mind to focus on Ishvara. One can light a pleasant smelling candle. A pious environment needs to be prepared for the mind to be able to attach to Ishvara. If a deity or Ishvara with human form is chosen as the mind's focal point, the mind will be able to think, feel, perceive, and sense the glory and attributes of Ishvara. Ishvara is described as the treasure of the best qualities. The mind is capable of not only concentration but also of absorbing Godly qualities like compassion, love, truth, non-violence, service, and dispassion. Concentration is called here as a mental worship to Ishvara, or *Upasana*.

If one regularly performs the prescribed concentration, one's concentration not only becomes stronger, but the mind becomes purified of ill-feelings like anger, hate, jealousy, envy, attachment, and aversion.

Concentration affects and shapes one's conscious behavior. Purification of the unconscious and maturity of emotions is the biggest outcome of Bhakti of Ishvara with attributes. Only Bhakti or concentration of mind on Ishvara can affect and purify the unconscious mind. Depression, anxiety, loneliness, and anger on trivial matters are very common in today's society. Drugs and pills can help, but cannot remove the underlying cause in the unconscious. Only Bhakti or concentration on Ishvara can remove the cause because Bhakti connects a human being to the indwelling cause of the universe.

The person doing regular concentration on Ishvara with attributes develops as a Bhakta. In other words, the consciousness of a person practicing concentration on Ishvara regularly shifts from that of an individual to that of a Bhakta. A person gains a life of belonging to Ishvara and finds himself the same as Ishvara in *Chaitanya* (i.e. Spirit). The person's thought stream moves, keeping Ishvara in the center. Concentration of mind is a conscious re-orientation of a person's energy to its cause, or *Tapas*. Thus, *Tapas* pacifies a person's mind and body with which it does all transactions in the world. Concentration of mind is not only helpful for one's spiritual upliftment but also in one's daily life. A great scientist or professional is great because of his mind's ability to concentrate and ability to see which others can't see with the fickle mind.

A saint is a saint because of his concentration of mind on noble virtues of humanity like compassion, love, service, non-violence, and truthfulness. Every person is a potential saint if Godly humanness is brought out by concentrating on Ishvara. Vivekananda started concentration when he was a little boy. We can see that Bhakti or concentration on Ishvara transforms a raw human being into a saint or Bhakta. A person who is mature in emotions and intellect can progress on the path of Ishvara. A person with troubled feelings and thoughts needs to first make his mind stable and relatively calm using concentration. Such a peaceful mind ready person can successfully meditate. Such a person's ego gets diluted because Ishvara is his father and mother. Such a person is cooperative, understanding, accommodative, can easily mix with others, and lives a life of bringing belongingness, warmth, intimacy, and love to the world. *Bhagavad Gita*[2] declares that such a Bhakta has no hatred for any being, is friendly, compassionate, without possessiveness, without doership, forgiving, and has a composed mind in pain and pleasure.

The first step in stabilizing happiness is a calm and cheerful mind reaped through regular concentration. If a mind is gathered, relatively free, and joyous, it can pursue meditation. One cannot become happy by the possession of wealth, health, family, fame, and power, but by an emotionally and intellectually matured mind purified by concentration. A human being experiences through the mind as the mind is acting as an instrument of experience. If the instrument of experience is agitated, or full of conflict and turmoil, whatever one experiences will be an unhappy experience. If a person is endowed with an unhappy mind, nothing matters. The best situations in the world or even heaven will trouble the person. Concentration of the mind means creating a relatively happy, free, and secure mind. Concentration done on Ishvara will create a sensitive and strong mind. Such a mind is imbued with trust, high morals, noble emotions of well-being, affection, well wishes for others, doing good to all, and is friendly to all.

Bhagavad Gita[3] gives an example of a person with a stable mind and whose mind is in its control, or *Atmavan*. Like a tortoise who can willingly withdraw its limbs when it wishes to, similarly a person with a concentrated mind can withdraw his mind and senses from its respective objects at will. Not only can he withdraw, but also he can put the mind and senses to a chosen object and can focus the mind to stay on the object for a longer period of time. This ability of a person is a preceding step of meditation. How can one reverse the mind to its source if one can't gather the mind? A life of progress in self-knowledge is a human life, while a life of merely breathing is the life of an animal with a human body. Generally, we ignore the mind and take care of the body.

Purifying the mind through concentration, or *Chitta Suddhi*, is the first need of every human being because the mind plays a key role in his development. The mind can act as either the cause of suffering if not treated at all or the cause of relief if it is concentrated on Ishvara. Too much progress of the physical world or body in the modern world and the neglect and avoidance of the mind results in the increase of mental disorders like hatred, anxiety, depression, loneliness, insecurity, and fear throughout society. How can one enjoy a good life if one has everything: house, insurance, degree, and family but one has an untreated raw mind? Human being's well-being lies in a gathered mind with noble qualities. In this regard, concentration and meditation of the mind must be regarded and prioritized as the foremost duty of a human being. A person does not tolerate a simple cold to his body and visits the doctor immediately, but keeps hatred, anger, anxiety, fear, loneliness without any worry! It's as if one has a large decorated house, but a backyard full of breeding snakes and insects. The current society has experienced violent and suicidal behavior due to disordered minds. By not understanding the role of mind in human evaluation, a person hinders his self-growth, and pays attention only to the body.

A human personality is mind and body, but ultimately resolves to *Chaitanya* (i.e. Spirit). Growth of self-knowledge is nothing but the removal of ignorance about our own personality makeup and finding the self as self of all, Ishvara, at the root of our personality tree. Concentration can prepare a mind which can discriminate and appreciate Ishvara in oneself and all.

---

1. 12.8
2. 12.13
3. 2.58

Chapter Twelve

DHARMA

*D*harma is a great means and a first step for self-knowledge and self-discovery. To recognize myself as Ishvara, I need to be a human being first. A human being becomes a human being because of his performance of the duties of a human being. Humanness is not given but needs to be brought out. Only a human body is given. Humanness is to be cultivated by the performance of duties as a human being. If one is given a human body, but does not have a set of values or Do's and Don'ts relating to humanness, then one is like an animal. The first step in self-knowledge is the recognition that "I am a human being," and I am supposed to think, feel, and act like a human being. Dharma is a universal set of values that uphold people and society, and that is recognizable in the intellect of a human being.

A human being first recognizes that "I am, and the other is," as well as "the other is related to me." I belong to the big picture rather than myself alone. Whenever I think, feel, and act, I need to treat the other half of myself, the world, with the same weight, respect, love, and dignity as I treat myself. A human being without human values is like a tree thinking that it is standing on its own feet, disregarding the soil on which it stands, the water that is sprinkled on it every day to nourish it, and the weather that is favorable to its growth. The recognition that my growth since childhood is dependent on other factors is the recognition of dharma. Feeling and acting on these values makes me human. I am responsible to Ishvara, society, and creation. In other words, I have some duties with respect to each one to perform. God is and is dwelling in me as the human spirit driving my body and mind. If I see an ordered creation around me, human intellect must infer a creator or Ishvara without choice. On the other hand, a human being without dharma does not understand that an order or laws govern the universe, even though the sun rises and sets every day and the moon appears only in the night. Even though I breathe without my intervention and even though the wind only blows and does not change its dharma or essential characteristic, a person without dharma ignores intellect and does not believe in Ishvara. Giving value to *Adharma* over dharma is disrespecting one's own mind and body. Recognition of dharma is the first manifestation or signature of Ishvara at the level of a human being.

A human being with strong values of humanness turns into a Bhakta who can appreciate Ishvara's creation and its order. Ishvara, in the form of Cosmic law or *Antaryamin*, rules the universe from within.

Humanness means adoring universal and eternal moral values and adhering to right conduct throughout life. Moral values bring order into a human being's emotions, thoughts, and actions. Hence the life of a human being becomes a melody or music of Ishvara. What are the values that make a human, human? One is gratitude to everybody starting with Ishvara who have played direct or indirect roles in one's life.

Truthfulness, faith, care, dignity, self-confidence, integrity, kindness, sympathy, love, non-violence, service, understanding, respect for others and creation, accommodation, trustworthiness, forgiveness, friendliness and detachment are the measure of a good human being's qualities. Adhering to these values makes one a universal man. Dharma is a connecting link between man and the universe. Dharma shapes a human being to be able to recognize Ishvara. Dharma makes cooperative living in the universe possible.

The right conduct in each situation makes one a follower and upholder of dharma. Understanding and playing one's part as a human being in the world properly and with priority creates a responsible human being who performs tasks assigned by Ishvara. Neglecting humanness is like not cooperating with Ishvara or not playing one's role in the drama assigned by the director. This creates emotional and physical turbulences in the human being. Relative peace and happiness at the human level is the result of performing dharma.

The *Bhagavad Gita*[1] proclaims that success in human life is doing what I am supposed to do. People complain that they work hard but cannot get an iota of mental peace. Mental peace is tantamount to performing human dharma and understanding my place in the big picture. It is not related to gaining wealth, health, fame, relationships, and power. That is why we see that some people are peaceful and happy, even though they are less achieved. A sage can be happy under its hut. The quality of human life depends upon its adherence to dharma and not on the quantity of objects that it possesses. A human being's mind and body follow the law of Ishvara as *Antaryamin*. To be a good human being must be the first goal defined for all human beings. Performance of dharma is the wellness and good health of a human being. Simple living, high thinking, and morals were the essence of Gandhiji's life. A few other great human beings were Vivekananda, Buddha, and Abraham Lincoln.

Two questions still need to be answered regarding a human being and dharma. The first one is: why does a human being not perform dharma even though he knows it? The second one is, how a person performing dharma, or *Dharmic* person, paves his way to self-knowledge.

Let us try the first question. Performance of dharma depends upon an individual's will. In every situation, there is always a choice of whether to adhere to human values or not.

The human being overrides the dharma because of the pressure of his own desires in the form of strong likes and dislikes. One must face the consequences due to the law of karma. The *Bhagavad Gita*[2]says a human being does not perform dharma because of his attachment, aversion, and resulting anger. Not performing dharma results in conflicts and clashes in one's own personality. Controlling one's self by oneself based on dharma is freedom while following one's attachment and aversions are inner bondage. As man's internals are executions based on dharma or universal order, when one ignores it, it creates division and strife in one's own personality or mind and body. Let us say that for short-term gain one cheats or hurts others. Then a knot is created in oneself because one always knows in his heart the guilt that one has cheated or hurt. How can one be happy if the mind is unhappy? Not knowing that the lives long self-degradation happens by ignoring dharma makes one perform against dharma for gratifying the demands of the ego. On the other hand, if one knows that performance of dharma will give peace and happiness, then one will always choose dharma. We also hear arguments such as 'I am cheating or being dishonest because others or society is like that'. This falls under the same ignorance about dharma. For creating a personality that is cheerful and restful, one needs to understand the importance of human values.

Let us try the second question. A *Dharmic* person's mind is at rest, relatively peaceful, and trouble free. A *Dharmic* person does not behave, think, feel whatever he likes, but always does, thinks, and feels what is right. It becomes one's habit to act on behalf of the dharma rather than one's ego demands, if it is against what is right. In this way, one's mind gets freedom from the tyranny of acting under the spell of ego. The performance of dharma based on one's own will result in reduced pressures from likes, dislikes, and uncomfortable feelings. One knows that Ishvara is an order in the universe as dharma and implies the unity of life. A spacious and peaceful mind has necessary strength now to discriminate between real and unreal. Now the mind becomes capable of discrimination, dispassion, self-inquiry, and concentration. To commit to a life of dharma is *Tapas* or the discipline of spiritual life.

Dharma keeps our motivation for a higher life burning and creates a longing for the realities of life rather than the animalistic enjoyment of life. Just as a tree bound to the earth grows, so human life established in dharma grows to self-knowledge. Dharma is like decorating the bride of a human mind to wed, join, and recognize Ishvara.

---

1. 18.46
2. 3.37

Chapter *Thirteen*

VALUE OF FAMILY LIFE

*F*amily life is a part of dharma and hence has a huge value in the gaining of self-knowledge. Here, one is not only a human being, but a human being playing the role of father, mother, son, daughter, grandfather, grandmother, husband, wife, uncle, or aunt. Marriage is not only a physical need, but more than that, it is a mental need. A human being always wants intimacy in the form of relations to feel that it belongs to somebody and somebody belongs to it. If we discard this necessity of mental need in the family, then family life has nothing more to offer in terms of the spiritual development of a human being. The feeling of belonging to someone and being cared for is satisfied by the family life. The family life is extended to friends. Thus, family life covers family and friends. The family institution is a platform for the growth of human qualities and values. The family responsibility is responsibility out of love, and hence one does not feel the burden of it. Family teaches a life of belonging, and relation based on common father and mother.

Family life is willingly accepted slavery of love. If one finds that roles and personalities attached to it make them slave in spirit, then one should stop playing as it degrades one's spirit and makes family life worthless. In family life, one becomes aware of one's duty, plays that role in the family, and does so with intimacy and love. One learns to willingly work for their loved ones. For example, a wife cooks for the family without any reward or expectations. Father and mother work tirelessly to make a comfortable living for the family. Kids are raised without expectations and educated until they become responsible for themselves. One's ego softens and learns a brand new dimension of oneself as family verses only oneself. One widens one's horizon of intimacy and duty to family and hence grows in spirit. One's hard personality learns to yield for their intimate ones. One learns to accept other personalities irrespective of their nature, age, education, gender, and lives under a common bond of elders. If I am a father and I perform my fatherly duties with love, then over time, I have widened and grown in love and spirit of Ishvara. One should play the role until it is comfortable and does not become burdensome.

A human being, to grow in noble qualities of a human being, needs a supportive environment and place of practice. On what platform can one learn human qualities like gratitude, love, sympathy, trust, forgiveness, service and taking care of each other? It is as if one wants to grow as a good doctor then one needs to work in a hospital. Similarly, family is a platform to train and educate human beings' desires, emotions, thoughts and actions to grow in the direction of intimacy, respect, humbleness, love, care, and wisdom. Intimacy that is experienced in family life is Ishvara himself in the flavor of intimacy. This pure, learned intimacy is then extended to friends and society, creating a harmonious and co-operating society based on family.

Generally, a person remains busy with career, similarly oriented friends, or in himself and neglects the family because he finds no spiritual importance in it. In general, a person uses his family to survive and adjust. Spending time and doing various activities, sharing emotions, and supporting each other in the family is time well spent. Because family is a dharma of a human being, family time satisfies all emotional needs and creates an emotionally healthy human being. Loneliness, anxiety, disappointments, and frustrations like mental deformations are automatically corrected in a person living a good family life. The biggest issue of personal security will go away if a person develops family feelings.

Ishvara is the head of the family because he is the common origin of all Jivas, based on karma, that have come together in the family. The law of karma is dharma, and Ishvara presides over that. If I understand that my specific family members are due to my close connection to them, due to the law of karma and hence Ishvara, then the family is seen as Ishvara given family. Family is a platform for self-growth and is the manifestation of the love of Ishvara in the form of fatherhood, motherhood and so on. Various flavors of Ishvara's love are experienced like a husband and wife's love for each other, parental love, and siblings love. This bond of Ishvara is experienced in each role of family life if members are aware that family love belongs to the love of Ishvara. Thus, due to the common bond of Ishvara, family is united in goal, feelings, thoughts, and enjoys together.

This understanding is the vision of Bhakti where each family member is intimate with each other based on Bhakti based love. With this vision comes understanding, forgiving others, and accommodating others when they lack in something. More closeness brings another issue of strong attachment and aversion due to separate qualities and shortcomings of different family members. In close-ness, I would naturally want to command my own and forget that they are the same human beings as me. Each role in a family is dignified and deserves proper respect and love.

Relating to each family member properly in accordance with its role creates a harmony and order in the family. Like a drama, each role plays and relates according to the script assigned by the director to bring out the drama. If each role in drama forgets or discards, their role and says that I am the same individual as others, then the drama stops. Ishvara as a director has assigned the roles and I am playing my role with enthusiasm and love. This vision becomes the basis of a successful family institution. Family life is tough when minds from different cultures are gathered in a family. All difficult problems can be solved with the vision of Bhakti based love. Love without Bhakti, itself turns into attachment and aversion and creates a problem in the spiritual development of a human being. One performing family dharma becomes Bhakta and appreciates Ishvara as dharma is truly living life. For example, if a child is born, the family can think that it is a child given by Ishvara and hence, each step of raising the child is naturally full of sacredness in the family.

A caution while growing on the family platform is necessary. The family should not become a place of sensual pleasure and party. It should be treated as a spiritual discipline leading to Ishvara. Hence, it should become a place of restraint or *Tapas* and platform of development to higher happiness. It should not become a place where the only thing talked about is games, movies, sightseeing, and food. This is the devaluation of the great family institution and human life. *Bhagavad Gita*[1] cautions a human being like a mother of humanity to not overindulge in senses and to restrain food, games, movies, and wandering habits.

The whole family needs to be educated with the vision of Bhakti based love. The thought of family's sacredness and connection to Ishvara needs to be shown logically using the law of karma to each member of the family. After learning this divine family feeling from family, it must be expanded to include the whole world. Bhakta looks at the world as his family. The family creates a loving, understanding, and forgiving personality with which individual and society can progress in a cooperating environment.

From family life, I learn that I am not self-made, but I am who I am because of others contributing to my life, starting from Ishvara, parents, siblings, uncles, aunts, friends, and environments. Without these contributing factors, I would not have been what I am today. Truly seeing this, my life becomes the basis of love of Ishvara. This is the value that family life provides for each of us.

Cultivated love and intimacy from the family must be channelized to its source, Ishvara. This softened personality needs to resign in its source and find complete happiness and love in the source of love and intimacy, Ishvara. It prepares us for the final knowledge that the source of oneness and love is the self of all, Ishvara alone, which is the self of mine as well. It is through the medium of family that I am experiencing love or the universal being. Initially, intimate relations start with expectational love, but gradually one understands that love or intimacy can never be asked for or found as an object in a person, it is the self alone that is known as love. It is only Ishvara's love that is invoked through the medium of each relationship. That is why love can only be distributed, celebrated, and why one needs to go into the direction of love without expectations. Although, in order to reach this understanding, one must follow the dharma of its role properly and consistently.

---

1. 6.17

Chapter Fourteen

DAILY PRACTICE

*S*adhana, daily practice or disciplined effort is necessary for self-knowledge, just as it is for other types of knowledge. We are dealing with the human mind and body, which includes current habits, impressions, desires, thoughts, and actions. Our aim should be to make a desirable change that makes our mind and body more conducive to gaining self-knowledge. Disciplining the mind and body is necessary to lessen or remove obstructions to self-knowledge. This practice that one should do is not to attain the self as the self is already attained. It is to remove the cover of self-ignorance or avidya veiling the self-evident self as Ishvara. If I practice daily certain helpful methods, then self-knowledge becomes accessible to me. A musician always tunes his instruments and rehearses before the show to get the desired music. The *Bhagavad Gita*[1] says that repeated practice or *Abhyas* and dispassion or *Vairagya* is necessary to create a conducive mind for self-knowledge. Commitment to daily practice is necessary.

As a human being we only delve into objective experiences that our senses, mind, body, and world provide to us. We delve throughout life in perishable experiences and lose sight of the imperishable self of the perishable. For example, we earn money and enjoy all the luxuries that it can provide. However, all that perishes in time, including money and health. Sometimes we do analyze the experiences, but of the world as we think of it. Sadhana or daily practice is a special time allocated for analyzing our experiences in the light of Vedant through self-inquiry and discrimination, reaching an experiential understanding of Ishvara as the self of all. Sadhana is a way to churn out the imperishable self from perishable objective experiences. Ignorant people joke about sadhana or the self because they are too far away in their experience and knowledge to even ascertain the imperishable self. Thus, they deny their own ultimate well-being and potential as a human being.

We have already described the means of self-knowledge. Let us see if we can make a meaningful daily routine or spiritual diet out of it so that one gets fulfilled. Although this is just one example routine, one needs to tailor it according to their own schedule.

In the morning, the mind is peaceful, fresh, and predominated by Sattva. Let us put the fresh mind first into the Ishvara. We can do discrimination between real and unreal, self-inquiry, meditation, concentration, any one of these, or all of these in the morning depending upon where I am is in terms of self-knowledge. Pacifying the mind and turning it in the right direction is *Tapas*. First, morning time needs to be preserved for Ishvara, the self of all. The mind just got out of nowhere as we woke up. This becomes a natural connecting time for the mind to see its own essence. This needs to be done regularly and with a cognitive outlook. A cognitive outlook is necessary because it means to keep Ishvara, the reality with form or without form, in view rather than anything else. Scientists bring out wonders by using a cognitive outlook on nature. Here, we keep a cognitive outlook not for nature, but for that which resides as nature. The *Ishavasya Upanishad*[2] says all these things are Ishvara alone. In order to preserve my daily practice, I should sleep early in the night and should stay away from night parties. Understanding that these means of self-knowledge are very powerful leads to self-discovery of self as *SatChitAnanda*.

Then, I go to work to make a living and come back in the evening. It is family time or friend's time for those who do not have a family. We need to spend a couple of hours satisfying our family dharma. Understand that laughing, taking care, supporting, sitting, or doing any activity with family members is worthwhile as it satisfies our emotional nature and develops the best of human virtues in us. If somebody asks me to be humble, I cannot be humble even if I want to be. I need to have learned humility through the family institution. As a human being, one needs an answer to one's emotions, which one finds living a healthy family life that nourishes the soul. Family members that meet just at the dinner table, just say 'hi, hello', are always busy with their cell phones and laptops, or respond only to the family's practical needs cannot grow into relationships and feel the intimacy of Ishvara. Family, or intimate relationship, is a great instrument given to us to develop into love and intimacy. Due to the ignorance of the greatness of the family, family becomes useless or even turns into pain of living together. Two basic qualities need to be learned by a human being: being independent enough to stand on one's own feet and being able to live together with increasing love and intimacy. Family institution develops a human being with both of these basic qualities.

One can arrange *Satsang* for a couple of hours in a week. One can set up some time for spiritual or devotional activities through some established institutions. A family prayer time, either daily or for a few days of the week, is very good practice. Once in a while, community or social activity with a spiritual goal is helpful.

Before going to bed, if we read or hear something related to the non-dual self or Ishvara, it will last even in our dreams. No other thoughts can come. Sleep is any way as if merging back to self, then why not hear or read about self or Ishvara at bedtime? Self is churned by analyzing one's own experiences, because the self is the root of all experiences or *lokan*.

Vedant gives techniques to analyze these experiences, and by following these techniques, we become aware of our self as shared divinity. In order to learn these techniques, we need to read and understand the original books or commentaries written on *Upanishads* and *Bhagavad Gita*, the source of non-dual knowledge or Vedant or *Shruti*. If we cannot do that, we can listen to a non-dual teacher at this time before going to sleep. After all, our story is the story of the tenth man.

This is just an example schedule or practice. One can make one's own schedule, but it requires embedding all means of self-knowledge during some time of the day to progress in self-knowledge. For example, if I just read or listen and do not do any meditation or self-inquiry or vice versa, I cannot progress far. If I do both of these, but do not relate to the world from the seat of love or Ishvara, then self-knowledge cannot be complete. Whatever I learned or discovered needs to be expressed through thoughts, desires, and actions without any hindrances.

The Prasna Upanishad[3] mentions faith in source books and teachings on the topic of non-duality or *Shradha*, disciplined effort or *Tapas*, commitment and persistence in self-knowledge or commitment to the truth, reality or *brahmacharya* leads to success.

Spiritual unfoldment of self is the gradually growing clarification of our experiences. Like, if I see a man from a distance, I may not recognize him at first look, may mistake him for somebody else, or may not recognize at all. Instead, I go sufficiently near to him while wearing my glasses, I can recognize him clearly and rejoice. This is going near to myself is what daily practice or *Sadhna* allows me to accomplish.

---

1. 6.35
2. 1.1
3. 5.3

Chapter Fifteen

SATSANG

The company of the wise, or *Satsang,* is another powerful means of self-knowledge. Because the mind is an important tool in gaining self-knowledge, it requires the proper environment or company to acquire the right tendencies, practices, and direction. The mind and senses have a natural tendency towards materialism because they face outwards. The company of the wise can help the mind turn inwards and infuse it with *Sattva.* If I am in good company, my mind will be influenced and spiritually uplifted because the mind is receptive. Although some seekers know the right direction, they could not travel the spiritual path because of close association with the directionless, aimless, and materially oriented people. A company of minds that are attached to sensual pleasures and ego gratifying activities pull down each other. With friendship for pleasure, eating, drinking, and making merry, it is impossible to aim at the knowledge of the cause of the world, or Ishvara. If there is a good pull in the direction of Ishvara, the mind will become one's friend. Otherwise the mind acts as a foe in attaining self-knowledge. *Amritabindu Upanishad*[1] says for a man, mind is the cause of bondage and mind itself is the cause of liberation. Mind attached to sense objects is the cause of bondage, and mind detached from sense objects is the cause of liberation.

Satsang is the association with the truth and can take many forms. It can be a group of spiritually oriented people regularly meeting to read, listen, and discuss *Shruti* or Vedant. It can be headed by a guru who is spiritually enlightened and can guide a group of seekers to reality. Regular retreats of guru can be attended as a form of *Satsang*. Satsang can even simply be the company of a spiritual friend with whom frequent discussions of reality or Ishvara are held. The *Bhagavad Gita*[2] says that in always sharing, or teaching, and describing Ishvara's knowledge, the seekers rejoice and totally satisfy themselves. *Satsang* can be joining a spiritual organization, which is running various activities, with the aim of spiritual upliftment. Here is a word of caution. A person should not be emotionally attached to such an organization. He should not keep busy in growing and maintaining the organization while forgetting the true aim of *Satsang*. *Satsang*, in the simplest form, can even be regularly going to the countryside, riverbed, or mountain in nature and reading *Shruti* books or listening to a non-dual teacher's words. If a physical guru is present, a one-on-one, or one-on-few

Satsang is highly desirable and the most attractive form of *Satsang*. In this form of Satsang, one can openly ask questions regarding reality or the path to reality to an enlightened guru.

What effect does *Satsang* have on the mind? *Satsang* dehypnotize the mind and liberates us. *Adi Shankaracharya* in his *Bhaja Govindam*[3] explains it in very terse words. *Satsang* brings detachment or *Vairagya* in the mind, which in turn gives freedom from delusion. Such a free mind attains self-knowledge that is the cause of liberation while living. The mind is made up of *Sattva, Rajas,* and *Tamas.* Mind deconditioning needs to happen through the medium of *Satsang* to arrive at self-knowledge. An increase of *Sattva* and decrease of *Tamas* and *Rajas* quality is necessary to remove blockage of the mind. Because the mind is the main instrument through which the self is reflected. A mind dominated by qualities of *Tamas* and *Rajas* is highly unlikely to establish the cause of the universe, Ishvara, as the self. The company of good and wise people unknowingly turns the mind in the right direction of *Sattva* and devotion to Ishvara due to their influence or positive peer pressure. I know a great person who has attained greatness due to keeping his mind always absorbed in the good thoughts of *Shruti* and his guru throughout his life. Such is the life changing effect of *Satsang.* For example, look at Narendranath Datta after coming in company with Ramakrishna Paramahansa.

Satsang helps in correcting the errors in one's thinking process. One understands the glories of Ishvara. It helps in bringing new good qualities and takes one to the path of Ishvara. It helps one in knowing the way to Ishvara. Saints and sannyasins often meet along the way in a village, temple, or in *parikrama* (pilgrimage) with other people to glorify and discuss the knowledge of Ishvara. *Satsang* has a powerful effect of transforming the whole village if some saint or sannyasin is regularly doing *Satsang*. Generally, one should aim for a wiser and more virtuous friend for *Satsang* to be able to grow. A friendship based on devotion and thought for Ishvara can bring about a miraculous change in one's life and steer one towards the final destination of the human journey called liberation in life.

---

1. 2
2. 10.9
3. 9

Chapter Sixteen

STORY OF TWO BIRDS

*T*wo birds with beautiful wings were perched on the same tree. Both were best friends, although their characteristics were totally different. One bird was sitting on the highest branch while the other bird was jumping back and forth between the bottom and middle branches. The bird sitting below on the tree was eating the fruits and was dancing and screaming if the fruit was sweet and was throwing away if the fruit was bitter. The bird sitting on the top branch was peacefully looking at his friend without blinking. He was enjoying within himself without eating any fruits. The lower bird would frequently keep looking at his friend and would try to approach him, especially after he tasted a bitter fruit.

The above story occurs in the *Mundaka Upanishad*[1] and is highly relevant to the process of attaining self-knowledge.

The bird sitting on the lower branches is Jiva and his friend sitting on the top branches is Ishvara. Jiva is samsari and hence enjoyer and doer. He keeps himself involved in doing and enjoying the fruits of his action. Ishvara, with reference to Jiva, is the witness consciousness who is not interested in the fruits of action and just watches the Jiva dispassionately. Both the birds are friends, meaning that they are connected to each other as reflection and original.

Jiva, or personality, is the self, or pure consciousness, reflected or entangled in psychological and physiological processes, confused, and helplessly experiencing pain and pleasure. In other words, suffering is inevitable if self-knowledge is of a separate personality. Personality defines the self as "I am the doer" and "I am the enjoyer," which ties Jiva, or the self-conscious person, to psychological and physiological processes belonging to the mind and body. Jiva thinks that I own these psychological and physiological processes, or 'I am' is equal to these psychological and physiological processes. This tie makes him suffer endlessly in repeating cycles of pain and pleasure or jump up and down the tree of Samsara. Jiva considers himself helpless and unworthy.

Jiva starts pondering about his imperfect and incomplete situation and compares himself with the top bird, Ishvara, who is perfectly happy, calm, free, and lord. The attraction of perfecting one's self is built into a human being. It only needs to be brought out by discernment.

After discerning that I can be free from misery just like the bird sitting on the top branch, Ishvara, who is free and happy, I start on the path to self-knowledge with the help of guru and Shruti. Using all self-knowledge means available, I start approaching Ishvara and start getting stable peace and freedom.

The process of self-knowledge is nothing but coming out of the self-created turmoil of psychological and physiological processes with the clear knowledge of their essence. The clear knowledge is that one's self is the material and efficient cause of these processes. Let us take the human faculty of intellect as an example and its resulting stress. If Jiva's self-knowledge progresses as a result of spiritual practices, stress will not be caused. Why? Stress resides in the intellect. The cause of the intellect is Jiva's own self, which is the nature of pure consciousness or *Chaitanya* that is really without intellect. Discovering and understanding this does not allow stress to be created. Jiva's real nature is mere witness consciousness, or the top bird. Because the intellect has no independent existence of its own apart from the self, how can intellectual processes, resulting in stress, bind? Let us take another example where Jiva has a strong desire that makes him feel less or incomplete, without the attainment of the object of desire. If self-knowledge progresses, Jiva knows that fullness or completeness is one's own nature. The binding part of desire, longing for the object, is nullified. As a result, one does not feel incomplete if the desired object is not obtained. It then becomes the play of one's self as Ishvara. Lightning in the sky is a fleeting manifestation of static electricity. Similarly, psychological and physiological processes become the expression or manifestation of Jiva's self-effulgent self, which 'I am' is: *SatChitAnanda.*

This is how Jiva, the lower bird, approaches the top bird, Ishvara, and feels its innate lordship and freedom. In other words, Jiva becomes Ishvara as Jiva is a reflection of the original bird Ishvara.

Once self-knowledge as Ishvara, the self of all is attained, Jiva resolves to Ishvara as a reflection resolves to original. Then, involvement of the kind "I am the enjoyer" and "I am the doer" in the psychological and physiological processes goes away due to the removal of self-ignorance. Jiva's self-identity is no more invested in the psychological and physiological processes. Hence, binding power and limitations of mind and body become less and less felt while living until Jiva completely resolves himself to Ishvara, the top bird. Initially, these processes were unconsciously controlling Jiva due to the absence of self-knowledge.

Now the process of individuation or personality resolves, and hence, these processes are also resolved into Ishvara, with the understanding that they do not exist by themselves.

Let us understand the story of the two birds, the Jiva and Ishvara in-depth by thoroughly analyzing the nature of an individual.

1. 3.1.1,2

Part Three

NATURE OF AN INDIVIDUAL

Chapter Seventeen

THE POSITION OF A HUMAN BEING

*U*nderstanding the position of a human being while living the life of a human being is critical and inevitable. If I am unaware of my position as a person in the world, I can still live and pass my entire life. I can enjoy a few possessions, but I will never find the answers to my troubles, suffering, and agony. If I want to live a human life to its fullest potential, perfection, and beatitude, then I need to first adequately understand my position as a human being.

Let us look at the big picture of the position of a human being. As a human being, I recognize the world and myself as a person interacting with the world. As a human being, I am separate from the world and the world is separate from me. As a human being, I am an embodied person with mind and body. My identity is solely based on the mind-body complex. This is how I know myself. Let us call me – this aware person whose identity is based on a mind-body complex as a Jiva. From now on, let us refer to this conscious person, a Jiva or a human being. Jiva knows that I am here, and the world is there. One enormous capacity human life has is the capacity of doing and knowing. This capacity of knowledge and work makes me proud and allows me to live a pleasant life. I can do things and enjoy things. I perform actions and reap the fruits of my actions in terms of various pleasures. I am an enjoyer of various enjoyments that life can provide, and a proud doer of good and bad deeds. This mind-body complex based identity or Jiva is born someday and will die someday. In between, this person goes through the best and the worst experiences of life. The Jiva has an inner life that he is conscious of. General descriptions of such experiences are as follows.

I am happy. I am unhappy. I am elated. I am depressed. I am lonely. I need some space to be alone. I am getting old. I am young. I am sick. I am healthy. I am black. I am white. I am brown. I am angry. I am at peace. I am suffering. I am devastated. I am ok. I hate this. I love this. I am stressed. I am relieved. I am deaf. I am dumb. I am ignorant. I am a scholar. I am jealous. I have no peace. I am in fear. I have gray hair. The world is terrible. The world is wonderful. The world is like this or that.

The above repeating pairs of opposite experiences make up the inner life of a Jiva. I am happy sometimes, and I am sad at other times. I am sometimes elated and depressed at other times. I am lonely sometimes and overwhelmed by the world at other times. I suffer sometimes and am peaceful at other times. I enjoy sometimes and despise at other times. The world is good sometimes, and bad at other times. Jiva tries to weed out unhappiness from his experiences and wants to keep only happiness. Jiva tries to avoid pain and suffering from his experiences, but he cannot do that. As a result, Jiva feels helpless and his unconscious registers helplessness.

Jiva's life is a constant search for happiness and immortality. Jiva's experiences are full of uncertainty, insecurity, and fear. Jiva needs to constantly and repetitively amend the situations, relationships, and objects around him to make them conducive to happiness and security. Jiva is constantly tossed between pain and pleasure. Jiva constantly suffers attachment and aversion. He likes something, and he dislikes something. Jiva's object of like or dislike may be a person, situation, or even a color.

This is a picture of a relatively happy life of Jiva. Relative happiness and survival of a Jiva is subject to conditions around him and in himself. As human beings, we are limited by bodily limitations like aging, decaying, and dying. We are limited by mental deformations like attachment, aversion, envy, loneliness, depression, anxiety, anger, despair, and desire. Jiva's life is a life of continuous becoming. To become something new is a constant urge that drives the life of Jiva.

Jiva has countless desires. He constantly tries to fulfill desires by performing actions to become complete. Human life is engendered by the continuous urge to act based on one's own desires, which are in turn various attachment and aversion impressions in his unconscious mind called *vasnas*. This force of compulsion of karma is inevitable in human life. *"Karmanubandhini manushya-loke"*, says the *BhagavadGita*[1].

Thus, Jiva lives a life of continuous becoming by performing various actions to enjoy, fulfill and protect oneself. He enjoys good and bad situations based on the result of his own actions. Thus, unconscious mind based *vasnas* impelled desire, karma and results of karma forms a cycle of *sukha* and *dukha* for the Jiva. We call this cycle – *Samsara*.

Jiva carries a lot of mental complexes in his unconscious mind from previous lives and keeps gathering and adding to the accumulated store from current life experiences. As a human being, because I am self-conscious, I have a lot of complaints about the world and myself.

Jiva needs to constantly chase and acquire objects of his desire and preserve them to maintain his happiness. Jiva needs to constantly get rid of objects to preserve his happiness and security. Instant and immediate sense and ego gratification derived from objects of the world is the nature of Jiva. Objects of the world like people, situations and relations are continuously changing and perishable. Jiva's blind run after objects of his security and happiness finally frustrates and disappoints him.

As human beings, we are constantly trying to get rid of our limitations and endlessly trying to complete ourselves.

Even though Jiva is living a decent life of a wealthy, healthy, educated, insured and civilized member of a human society, still he feels something is yet to gain and not complete or missing from himself. Jiva continuously feels this littleness and dissatisfaction with himself, which becomes the cause of further actions to improve his fate. Jiva continuously tries to distinguish himself from the world and tries to get bigger and better than the world. Jiva is always in conflict with the world. He acts with the world or others with only a measure of self-interest. Sometimes Jiva acts with the world with enlightened self-interest so that others or the world do not threaten his existence.

Fear of death and desire to complete himself is ingrained in Jiva. Being a separate entity from the world, fear of survival is always at the back of Jiva's head. When an unexpected situation threatens Jiva's existence, this fear of self-destruction comes out and expresses itself in Jiva's actions, thoughts and feelings. Jiva wants more and more happiness and security. He finds happiness and security coming and going, but not staying forever. What will happen to me if I lose my job? What if I am infected by disease? Such concern for the future is always lingering in Jiva's mind.

Above is an in-depth analysis of human experience and what we do, on what basis we do, and why we do. This is the position of ourselves as a human being bound by *Samsara*. Jiva is bound by a cycle of birth and death, happiness and misery, doership and enjoyership, superiority and inferiority. Jiva helplessly suffers and is bound by the cycle of repeated actions or *karma* and enjoyments or *bhoga*. We are happy, but not enough; we are protected, but still vulnerable and can lose life anytime.

This position of ours as a human being can be compared to a sacred ficus tree as described in the *Bhagavad Gita*[2] called *Asvattha* with its roots upward and branches downwards. The tree here is a metaphor representing the ever-changing, repeating and undying cycles of *Samsara* with a root upward and hidden.

Is there a way out of this situation as a Jiva who is a *Samsari*? Is it possible to remove sorrow and suffering from human life? A human being who understands that his position is time-bound or of continuous change, space or body bound, and understands that the world of objects or others also limits him, will try to look for the remedy to the problem of *Samsara*.

---

1. 15.2
2. 15.1

Chapter Eighteen

PROMISE OF FREEDOM

*O*nce a self-conscious human being recognizes his limitations and understands that his relatively happy situation is subject to suffering and sorrow, he will start looking for the cure of the disease of *Samsara*.

Mental suffering and sorrow are unwanted patterns of mental modifications that occur in a self-conscious human being. They are keenly experienced, repetitive, and with no solution. *Dukh* and *Sukh* become constant companions in a relative plane of happiness for a Jiva.

Shruti or Vedant now becomes important and relevant because its purpose and subject is *BrahmaVidya*. *Brahma-Vidya* is a means of knowledge for the seekers of absolute freedom, happiness and immortality. The beauty of Vedant is that it never conflicts with a human being's rational faculty of *buddhi* or intellect, and instead, uses it to enhance the quality of human life to its ultimate destination of well-being known as *Param Padam*.

Vedant is a complete analysis of human experience and shows clearly what is generally missed by a human being is of highest importance in solving the riddle of *Samsara*.

Let us see how Vedant lifts a human being from a relative plane of happiness to an absolute plane of fullness and wholeness. Vedant starts with a vow of ultimate freedom or *Moksha* for a human being and fulfills it.

A human being is subjected to *Samsara* or birth, death, and sorrow, but who is this sufferer of suffering? Rather than looking elsewhere in the world, Vedant says to ask a question: who is unhappy? What is the nature of an individual to whom this suffering affects? What is the nature of the self? Vedant points us to the most forgotten element of human experience, the self of a human being. Vedant claims that knowing the self as it is in its full splendor will solve the problem of *Samsara*. *Atmavid Tarati Shokam* says *Chandogya Upanishad*[1]. The knower of the self frees himself from sorrow. The human intellect is subjected to ignorance or not-knowing until it gets educated. This ignorance is not so much of a problem as long as it is ignorance about other than oneself.

However, a special type of ignorance called self-ignorance forms the root cause of *Samsara*. This self-ignorance, or *Avidya*, forms the basic subjective limitation of human existence. In fact, *Avidya* is the root limitation of a Jiva out of which other limitations spring into existence. By ignoring the self, we kill the self and bind ourselves to *Samsara*.

It is the knowledge of the self that makes the difference from suffering to *Ananda*, from death to immortality and from fear to fearlessness.

At some point in life, I need to wake up and take this decision consciously to look in the direction of the self for my ultimate well-being. One has to face oneself, the conscious person, the experiencer of various experiences. The decision to pursue spiritual life can come after sufficiently discriminating and analyzing human life and its experiences. Spiritual life is not shying away from the secular life of a human being, but to enhance it and take it to its final destination. Imagine a four-story human house. Building the first story of a human house signifies the human effort of surviving or *Artha*. It signifies the effort after things such as food, shelter and clothes. Building the second story of a human house signifies the human effort of well-being, better conditions of living, and various pleasures and prosperity. The second story signifies efforts *Kama*. Building the third story of a human house signifies the effort spent on *dharma* or being a better human being who is virtuous, charitable, compassionate, loving and ready to serve the needy. Building the fourth and last story of a human house signifies the human effort towards winning the ultimate freedom or *Moksha*, eternal happiness, and immortality for oneself. In fact, after understanding the effort of *Moksha*, we come to understand that even in the form of *Artha, Kama, and Dharma* efforts, what we really want is *Moksha* only. *Moksha* is an all-encompassing effort in human life. The effort of *Moksha* can be understood as recovering or situating in one's own true nature rather than going somewhere from wherever one is, or experiencing something new, which is not experienced until now.

Moksha means to us that by finding out the real nature of the individual, we can conquer the highest battle of human life and get absolute happiness and immortality. The promise of the freedom from relative to absolute level of happiness and immortality lies in understanding myself properly with no vagueness and doubt with the help of Vedant.

In the *Bhagavad Gita*[2], *Arjun* declares that his delusion is removed after gaining the knowledge of the self by the grace of the Guru *Krishna*. *Krishna* imparted the Vedantic teaching to *Arjun* that led to the destruction of all doubts about the self. The result of self-knowledge is liberation while living or *JivanMukti*. The aspirant resolves himself as *Asamsari*, or free from *Samsara*, and the immortal self of all beings. The seeker regains remembrance of himself in full splendor (*Atma Smruti*).

A lost child deprived of his mother keeps crying. No toys can satisfy him until he gets his mother. Similarly, Jiva can never satisfy himself, even if he makes countless efforts of all kinds until he recognizes himself as *Shiva*. This recognition of *Jiva* as *Shiva* is gaining oneself or *Atma Labha*.

Let us inquire in-depth into the real nature of an individual with the help of Vedant.

---

1. 7.1.3
2. 18.73

Chapter Nineteen

KNOWER AND KNOWN

To understand the nature of an individual or Jiva, we need to understand what is meant by knower or *Kshetrajna* and known or *Kshetra*. *Bhagavad Gita*[1] dedicates an entire chapter to teach us how to discriminate between knower and known and arrive at the reality which exists as an individual.

As an individual, I know the world. This means I am the knower and what is known is the world. Field, known, or *Kshetra* is a field, range, or scope of someone who knows it. *Kshetra* is a place of cultivation of the fruits of what is being sown in the field by the knower of the field or *Kshetrajna*. An individual has the will and the power of doing to sow something in the field of the world and earn the rewards.

The *Bhagavad Gita*[2] says we need to discriminate properly between the knower and known to get an insight into the real nature of an individual. Let us divide our total human experience into these two entities: the knower and known. This body is a field or *Kshetra* and the one who knows the body is knower of the field or *Kshetrajna*. In other words, an individual is a combination of *Kshetra* and *Kshetrajna*. That is the way we look at ourselves. The way we see ourselves is as a soul or principle of intelligence contained in the inert nature or body. It is like a person living in the house. We call ourselves this combination of body and spirit. We refer to the body as me or say that I possess it. We include the body in our definition of ourselves as an individual.

If we pay attention to our experience closely, *Kshetrajna* or the knower internally knows the body and hence, we cannot combine these two totally different entities, the knower and known, into one. We are *Kshetrajna* or knower of not only the external world, but the internal body as well. If my body is sick, I know that. If my body is healthy, I know that too. The knower of an object must be different from the object. I am a knower of the body. I am not the body and neither do I possess the body, but *Kshetrajna* is obtained, reflected, or qualified by the body. From my definition of myself, I should exclude the body.

Let us look more closely at the nature of the *Kshetra*. The known or object of knowledge is always changing and continuously transforming. *Kshetra* includes all that varies, disappears, is inert and is subject to time, space and causation. On the other hand, the *Kshetrajna* knows that which changes and disappears and is a constant observer to what is observed. *Kshetrajna* is a conscious and constant element of our experience.

The nature of *Kshetrajna* is pure consciousness. *Kshetrajna* is naturally knowing what appears in it. A startling observation needs to be made about the nature of *Kshetrajna*. The *Bhagavad Gita*[3] says that *Kshetrajna* in all *Kshetra* is Ishvara and is only one and the same. *Kshetra* or fields are countless and many. In other words, the same and only *Kshetrajna* resides in the body of all beings. *Kshetrajna* is really Ishvara, the self of all. *Bhagavad Gita*[4] declares that the self of a human being is the self of all: *Sarva-Bhutatma-Bhutatma*.

I cannot include the *Kshetra* which I am aware of in my nature and make-up because both *Kshetra* and my nature are of opposite characteristics. One is aware while the other is inert. One is only one while the other is many. One is constant. The other is changing continuously. I am invariably present and conscious when knowing all transformations or variations of the fields. I am a witnessing function of pure consciousness, and fields are witnessed by me. Changes of the fields are not affecting me because I am a changeless witness: *Sakshi Chaitanya*. I am found to be the nature of pure self-revealing consciousness.

Now, the question is, what else is witnessed and illuminated by me other than the world and body? What about physiological *Pranas* or breath necessary for the functioning of the body? I know that I am hungry. I am tired. I know the modifications of *Prana*. So, *Prana* needs to be included in *Kshetra*. How about the five sense perceptions through which we know the external world which are taste, smell, vision, hearing, and touch? I know that I am deaf, or I can hear. I know that I am dumb, or I can speak. I know that I can see, or I am blind. That means senses of knowledge, or *Indriyas*, need to be included in *Kshetra*. What else can I know as an object of knowledge? It is now getting scary as we approach the mind and apply the discrimination of knower and known. The mind, with its all feelings such as attachment, aversion, pain, and pleasure are known to me. I am angry. I am depressed. I am happy. All modifications of mind or *Antahkaran vrittis* are known to me. That means the mind is also in the category of *Kshetra*. Let us go deeper into our nature as individuals. What about our reasoning faculty with which we are making this discrimination? "I know" and "I do not know" – both my knowledge and ignorance is known to me.

The *Bhagavad Gita*[5] says *Kshetra* includes the world, five elements, body, breath, senses, mind, intellect, ego, total *Ahankar* or *Mahat* and unconscious or unmanifest casual root matter or *Prakriti*.

Let us further inquire into *Ahankar* or ego sense.

---

1. 13
2. 13.1
3. 13.2
4. 5.7
5. 13.5

Chapter Twenty

EGO SENSE

e are applying discrimination of knower and known to all that we experience. We know that our essential nature is *Kshetrajna* or the knower of the field. Whatever is found to be the field of knowing or known, we have subtracted from our essential nature. Until now, we have removed the five elements, body, breath, senses, mind and intellect as not us.

Let us continue our inquiry into our real nature as an individual. When we look at the ego sense, it seems like I am looking at myself. Is this limited and empirical subject really me? If we examine our experience, ego comes and goes. We do not see ego present in deep sleep and not even when we are absorbed in peak moments of meditation or *Samadhi*. We do not find a trace of the ego when we are in nature and looking at the sea or mountain. Temporarily, we do not experience the ego being present.

So, ego is really an ego-idea: a thought that occurs in attribute-less pure consciousness. It is *Aham Vritti* that is the root of our personality. We are really a *Sakshi* or witness of *Aham* thought that occurs in us and we see it coming and going. In other words, ego sense also is *Kshetra* and not us.

The idea of ego in its nature is the idea of oneself as an agent. "I am a doer" and "I am an enjoyer" idea or *Aham Pratyay* is ego sense. This sense of agency does not belong to the self. It makes us an agent of knowing and doing. The ego-idea does the greatest mischief to us because it is a product of self-ignorance or *Avidya*. What is the biggest mistake or mischief ego sense causes us to make? Ego sense, in its root sense, is a connecting idea between the knower and known, or *Kshetra* and *Kshetrajna*. It makes us believe that we are this *bundle of desires, thoughts, feelings, breath and sensations.* We become this little personality made up of thoughts, desires, feelings, breath and sensations. We spend our whole life preserving and decorating our little self-image or personality. If anything happens to this self-image, it happens to us and we suffer.

Adi Shankaracharya in Vivekachudamani[1] beautifully describes the nature of ego sense. It is really a reflection of *Kshetrajna, Chit* or consciousness, in *Kshetra*. A reflection signifies pure consciousness, which is really attribute-less, but becomes possessed of the attributes of doership and enjoyership that really do not belong to *Kshetrajna*. This non-discrimination forms our subtle body, is the chief cause of suffering, and makes us *Samari*. It is this personality idea that ties us to *Samsar* or pain and pleasure. Like a reflection of the sun in water is tossed by the tides.

After inquiring this way between the knower and known, we should negate self as being an agent. As doership and enjoyership really belongs to *Kshetra* and not to *Kshetrajna*.

How is ego manifesting? Ego sense is a "variable I" or actor which takes a role based on current adjuncts it associates with. *Aham Pratyay* or ego manifests itself as a thinker, feeler, enjoyer, doer, hearer, perceptor, smeller, and tester. Just like an actor who wears different costumes at different times and speaks various dialogues based on the role. Ego is *Vikari,* or changing, and hence belongs to *Kshetra* as *Kshetra* by nature is *Vikari* or changing. Ego sense, or this physio-psychological personality, keeps performing various actions and eating the fruits of his actions. Fruits in the form of pleasure satisfy him and fruits in the form of pain make him suffer.

We are really a knower or illuminator of an agency idea; it is something that is known to us, but not us. The agency idea is something that occurs in us like streams occur in water. It can't affect us in any way, just like the characteristics of the stream do not affect the nature of water. I am neither an enjoyer nor a doer and free from both.

Bhagavad Gita[2] describes that pure consciousness obtains a temporary status of doer or *Karta* and enjoyer or *Bhokta* in relation to Kshetra. This self-identity based on the mind-body complex is a mistaken identity and the root cause of *Samsara* or suffering of an individual. Ego sense disappears when its attributes are negated. Just like if an actors' costumes and the dialogues are negated, the actor goes away and the real person shines. Pure knowing or *Kshetrajna* plus *Kshetra* creates the ego notion or *Aham Vritti*: a person made of thoughts.

At the level of *Buddhi* or intellect, this *Aham Buddhi* needs to be falsified. Here, pure consciousness recognizes itself as a reflection in *Kshetra* as *Chit Pratibimba*. *Kshetrajna* is really all these reflections in different *Kshetra*, like a sun reflected in various ponds. "I am separate from Ishvara." This separate sense goes away once the subtle discrimination about the nature of knower and known is made about ourselves. "I am separate from Ishvara" is replaced by the self of all or *Sarvatma*.

All thoughts, desires, feelings, sensations, actions, and relations in the world of such an individual follow the self of all and not the *Aham Buddhi* or ego sense. Such an individual, because of its recognition of the same self of all, always remains busy with the well-being of all. One thing needs to be clear here is that this non-discrimination or mistake is what makes us this reduced or limited self and it is negated or corrected at the level of cosmic intellect, total intellect, or *Samsti Ahankar,* or *Mahat*. The difference between Jiva and Shiva is adjunct based and hence not real. Right knowledge is that we are essentially *Kshetrajna* and our self is the self of all. Here, the individual self is replaced by the self of all. The same "I" that was known before to us as an individual or *Vyasti,* now, really is recognized as the same and only "I" or *Kshetrajna* in all personalities. Personalities are different – that is fine and true – but their "I" is one and the same. *Bhagavad Gita*[3] declares that a person who sees the same self Ishvara everywhere does not injure himself by himself and reaches the highest end of freedom, happiness, and immortality.

Without knowing the same self, one creates a wall of separation between himself and other persons, himself and Ishvara, and himself and the world.

---

1. 186,187
2. 13.21
3. 13.28

Chapter Twenty-One

INNER SELF

We started with our common experience of the world that "I am the subject" and "I know or experience the object." Then, we started investigating the subject and found that even the ego is an object of consciousness and cannot be considered as self or subject. Let us look more into the nature of *Kshetrajna* since we have already negated all objects of experience from our experience and left with only inner self or subject or *Kshetrajna* or *Pratyak Atma*. Understand that unmanifest or *Avyakt Prakriti* is also an object of knowledge.

The name inner self or *Pratyak Atma* is because the self is inner to all that we described as the field or *Kshetra*. The inner self of us is made up of pure consciousness or *Chaitanya Svarup*. The attributes-less pure consciousness is *not an object*.

We establish the existence of the world by perceiving it in terms of whether a perceived object "is" or "is not." For example, a tree is there, because I see it or feel it. If we cannot establish the existence of the object through the faculties of our direct perception or indirect perception of inference, then we say that an object does not exist.

What if an entity cannot come under this range of being perceivable, but it exists with certainty? That is the case about our inner self. The inner self of ours is not an object and cannot be objectified or perceived, but it still exists because it is self-evident and self-existent. We all know that "I am" and we know without using mind and with full certainty that "I am." The inner self is beyond the scope of the senses and mind. This knowledge of "I am" with its existence is not an objective knowledge. The inner self is not known by a general way of knowing as "I am the subject knowing this object". Inner self is beyond the categories of "Sat" or "Is" and "Asat" or "Is not" but the very basis of anything that exists or does not exist. The *Bhagavad Gita*[1] declares that by knowing this self one gains immortality or freedom from time. The *Bhagavad Gita* declares the inner self of man to be *Brahman* or the reality of the universe. In other words, if we know ourself as not made up of mind and body, but of pure consciousness and existence through this discrimination based on human experience, then we become liberated from the jaws of time or death.

Inner self is self-luminous or *"Svaym Jyoti"*. Inner self is *Chit Svarup* or knowledge form. Let us understand a bit more clearly this statement of *Bhagavad Gita*[2]. In the daylight, the sun illumines the objects of the world. But how does the sun or the source of light become known? Well, it is through our eyes. Based on the testimony of our perception, we know the sun. So, the sun depends on our perception of being existent. Without the mind, even senses cannot reveal the object of knowledge. If my mind is elsewhere, I cannot notice you even though you are in front of me. Thus, the senses become the object of knowledge of the mind. Similarly, the mind also falls short of being self-luminous. It is the inner self of us or *Pratyak Atma* who sees the mind and no one sees the inner self. That is why it is named as the most inner to all and our essential nature. Thus, the inner self is the only one who knows itself, or is self-revealing, or is the light of lights. The light in objects, the light in sun, moon, fire, stars, and the light in speech, senses, and mind, are nothing but different beams of only one self-luminous light of the inner self. It is the inner self of us beaming through all the fields or *Kshetra*. The nature of our self is existence, knowledge and happiness – *SatChitAnanda*. Thus, we found our inner self as *never ceasing seer* or *Drik* nature.

---

1. 13.12
2. 13.17

Chapter Twenty-Two

KNOWN IS KNOWER'S BEING

*K*shetra or field is a generalized term used to denote all that is changing and knowable, which includes starting with the body and ending in the unmanifest including our personality. *Kshetrajna* or knower on the other hand is not subject to time, without attributes, and in the form of absolute existence, knowledge, and happiness. Now, the question arises, what is the connection between the knower and known? For an earnest seeker of reality, this is like a fork in a spiritual road. This division of unchanging *Purusha* and changing *Prakriti* needs to be resolved for the total freedom of Jiva.

We began ourselves as an individual with a specific mind-body complex and came up to the point after discriminating that we are essentially *Kshetrajna* or *Pratyak Atma* whose nature is found to be existence, knowledge and happiness or *"SatChitAnanda"*. Self of pure consciousness is already found to be the sole reality of the universe as an absolute existence. Then, this changing aspect called *Kshetra* is a dependent existence or *Upadhi* or adjunct of self and hence non-separate from him. *Kshetrajna* is the truth of *Kshetra* and does not form two parallel realities. Consciousness or *Chaitanya* himself, with respect to the knowable, gets the name of the knower or *Kshetrajna*. Ishvara is both the subject and the object of knowledge. *Kshetrajna* is the truth of Ishvara or his essential nature, and *Kshetra* is his self-becoming or *Svabhav*. The being of known is actually the knower's being. *Bhagavad Gita*[1] mentions these two natures, one is essential or *Para,* and the other is becoming of it or *Apara.* Ishvara is a great resolver, meeting point, and resolving point of the knower and known. The pure consciousness, *Satta* or the existence of *Kshetra,* takes the name of *Kshetrajna* in relation to *Kshetra*. Therefore, *Kshetrajna* and *Kshetra* are not two separate and independent realities. The creation starting from unmanifest or *Avyakta* and ending in the body is devoid of existence and is only name and form. Just like streams, bubbles, foam, and tides form in water, the whole creation springs up in the pure conscious being or Ishvara without any effort.

The resolution of *Kshetrajna* and *Kshetra* is the dying of the dualistic human experience because the subject-object difference becomes unreal. Ishvara or *Kshetrajna* is realized as the cause of the universe or *Kshetra*. Ishvara is known as an efficient and material cause of the universe. He is an efficient cause in the form of knowing *Purusha* and material cause in the form of an unchanging but appearing as changing aspects called *Prakriti*. The aspirant can verify, in his own experience, that experience is nothing but the field of his own essential nature of awareness. The human experience is nothing but the conscious being Ishvara. This dualistic and transactional experience is nothing but a varying manifestation of non-dual Ishvara.

When from pure *Kshetrajna*, the knowing aspect is ignored, discarded, or forgotten, the subject-object duality becomes real and *Kshetra* appears as real, continuously changing, and transforming reality. The conscious being Ishvara is both knowing or *Chit* and being or *Sat*. After resolving these seeming two different aspects of the same reality, the human experience becomes *Ananda* or absolute happiness. Our self is essentially free from subject-object and is the nature of non-dual consciousness. The resolution of subject and object is *Ananda*. This non-dual experience of our self, where subject and object are resolved into each other without any trace left is the culmination of experience and also is called as the dying of the experience or *Anubhav Avasanam*. *Prakriti* forms an adjunct of the self to appear as the world. Knowing that *Kshetra's* being lies in *Kshetrajna*, *Kshetra* loses itself and hence *Kshetrajna* also resolves. Pure consciousness knows itself and cannot be divided into subject and object of knowledge. For *Atma-Chaitanya* or attributes-less pure awareness, he is both the subject and the object simultaneously.

Bhagavad Gita[2] declares that one who sees that differences in beings have their existence rooted in the one and from that one their projection, then one realizes *Brahman*. Not only the variegated world is non-separate and derives its existence from the self, but the self is the world. Ishvara is both the efficient and the material cause of the world. Ishvara is the self of all. The world is a manifestation of Ishvara.

---

1. 7.5
2. 13.30

Chapter Twenty-Three

JIVA IS ISHVARA

The connection between the *Kshetrajna* and the *Kshetra* becomes the cause of suffering or *Samsara* for the Jiva. Dissociation, or removing the connection between the soul and nature, releases the soul from the bondage of nature. Let us understand why the discrimination between the *Kshetrajna* and the *Kshetra* results in the liberation of a soul from the entanglement of nature.

Let us take an example of Jiva's experience: "I am ugly". Jiva always feels less and shys away from others because of this experience. Here, "I am" is *Kshetrajna* and ugly is the body or *Kshetra*. A characteristic of the body, specifically ugliness, is falsely superimposed upon *Kshetrajna*, which is the nature of pure consciousness. Similarly, the *Kshetrajna*'s consciousness and existence are given to the body. Vedant sees this error as mutual superimposition or

Anyonay Adhyasa where the characteristics of one thing is mistaken for another, and vice versa. Here, characteristic marks of *Kshetrajna* and *Kshetra* are mutually superimposed because of a lack of discrimination on the part of Jiva causing *Samsara*. This connection between the *Kshetrajna* and *Kshetra* is falsely assumed due to ignorance of their natures. The *Bhagavad Gita*[1] declares that the whole nature of mobile and immobile creation requires both the *Kshetrajna* and *Kshetra* combined, where the pure consciousness exists in many names and forms. The mind and body of beings are the names and forms where one and the same *Kshetrajna* resides. Jiva needs to carefully distinguish himself from the names and forms and recognize himself as Ishvara and the support, sustenance, and resolution of all names and forms of the *Kshetra*.

First, *Kshetra* is weeded out from *Kshetrajna* from Jiva's experience after understanding their characteristics and correcting the error of mutual superimposition. Then, this *Pratyak Atma* of pure consciousness is recognized as the cause of *Kshetra*, which resolved *Kshetra* into its truth, *Kshetrajna*.

Now, *Kshetrajna* has gained the name of Ishvara because of its casual adjunct of being an efficient and material cause of the creation. First, discriminating self or *Atma* from not-self or *Anatma* and then resolving *Anatma* in *Atma* solves the riddle of Jiva's suffering. Jiva is now clearly recognized as Ishvara. *Bhagavad Gita*[2] points out, this result of the liberation of Jiva from the bondage of nature.

---

1. 13.26
2. 13.34

Chapter Twenty-Four

REALIZING THE INNATE FREEDOM

*J*iva's strong identification with limited adjuncts or *Upadhi* and its qualities or *Gunas* makes him inherit the qualities of the limited adjuncts or *Upadhi*. As a result, Jiva thinks and feels that I am the mind-body or I have the mind-body. This identification makes him suffer the consequences resulting from this identification and veils Jiva's true nature as Ishvara.

As a result, Jiva's experience becomes, "I am unhappy," "I am stressed," "I am disturbed," "I am angry," "I have no peace," "I am alone or lonely"… etc. Because these experiences become repetitive, Jiva tries to increase the limits of the mind-body by trying various available means to stay safe and healthy. Such efforts can give at the most temporary relief to Jiva. Because the adjunct of the mind-body itself is limited and bound by space, time and causation, Jiva is bound to suffer their limits. However Jiva tries to realize freedom, the limited can never turn into unlimited or infinite, which he really seeks.

Jiva has a choice to make here, either suffer endlessly from death to death or gain self-knowledge and realize the innate freedom as Ishvara.

Status of Jiva is like a blindfolded man left in a diamond quarry. Even though he is rich, he feels poor. How does the gaining of self-knowledge turn the table for Jiva from limited to limitlessness? Let us understand through an example. When an actor performs the role of Ravana, the king of Lanka, he dresses up, speaks the dialogues, and walks and talks like Ravana. After the drama is over and even in the midst of performing, the actor performing the role of Ravana does not feel shame, arrogance, the cruel behavior of Ravana, and even allows himself to die as Ravana on the stage happily. The only sole reason why an actor does not inherit the qualities of Ravana in his life is that he knows that his true nature is not Ravana, but Ravana is a taken role by him. Having this self-knowledge about his real identity, an actor does not get affected by the attributes of the role he assumes. On the other hand, an actor enjoys various roles and their limitations.

Let us take Jiva's experience, "I am stressed". Here, Jiva's identification with the limited adjunct or *Upadhi* of intellect causes stress. But once Jiva knows that he is a stress-free pure awareness or *Suddha Chaitanya*, stress, which is a quality of the intellect, can't be inherited from the intellect to him. Hence, Jiva feels peace amid stressful and tenuous situations.

Bhagavad Gita[1] dedicates two verses to explain the result of gaining self-knowledge is the realization of the innate freedom of Jiva. After gaining self-knowledge, even though Jiva is situated in the mind-body, he does not get affected by their qualities and limitations. This path of self-knowledge is the only means for the Jiva to discover himself as Ishvara and as a result realize his innate freedom. This innate freedom is what Jiva is always seeking for and aiming for all of his various activities.

Realization of the innate freedom means ascertainment of the self, which is beyond the productive power of *Karma*. As a human being, we are driven by the force of Karma. Under the compulsion of Karma, Jiva keeps on performing various activities throughout his life. As a result, Jiva gathers merits or *Punya* and demerits or *Papa*, which becomes the cause of future births.

This is described in the *Bhagavad Gita*[2] as attachment to *Prakriti* born qualities becomes Jiva's cause of future births in higher or lower species of life. To realize the innate freedom as Ishvara means understanding that compulsion of *Karma* belongs to *Kshetra* or *Prakriti*, not to the self. As human beings, when we find something beyond and at the source of *Karma* itself as our own self, then we realize our innate freedom and rediscover the status of Ishvara. Otherwise, our self-knowledge does not go further than a doer of deeds and that makes us keep gathering merits and demerits and perpetuates the cycle of *Samsara*. *Bhagavad Gita*[3] describes this way of realizing our innate freedom and makes us free from the status of the doer. Realizing that it is our self that gains the temporary status of the doer with reference to *Prakriti*, who is self's own power, makes us free from the bonds of the *Karma*. *Karma* is a continuous activity, or dynamic process found as the mind and the body. *Karma* is a reproductive power that binds a human being initially until not knowing its source, sustenance, and resolution are the human being's self.

Karma is an urge to produce something new, sustain something existing, change something to a different form and name, and go somewhere from where one is right now. As we have a mind-body, we are always busy with continuous actions of various kinds and producing various results. *Moksha* is nothing but gaining this freedom from compulsion of *Karma* so that even while performing *Karma*, it does not bind us, but becomes a means of expression of our innate freedom as Ishvara. *Bhagavad Gita*[4] declares such a person, even though continuously performing *Karma* because of the absence of doership or ownership of *Karma*, does not really see himself doing anything. He becomes free from the burden of *Karma*.

---

1. 13.31,32
2. 13.21
3. 13.29
4. 5.8

Chapter Twenty-Five

THE SELF OF ALL

We have said that our self is made up of pure consciousness or *Kshetrajna* and everything else is inert *Kshetra*. It means that our mind-body joins with all mind-bodies. We do not identify with a single mind-body anymore. Moreover, we already said that this inert *Kshetra* derives its existence and consciousness from our self and seems as if independently existing and conscious of itself. Also, we said that *Kshetra* is nothing but a manifestation of our self who is made up of pure consciousness and existence or *SatChitAnanda*. This makes our self as the self of all or *Sarvatma*.

The *Bhagavad Gita*[1] beautifully describes the self of all as having hands, feet, eyes, mouths, ears and heads on all sides and pervades them. The self shines by the functions of the senses, yet without senses, unattached and sustains them. The self being devoid of attributes, experiences the qualities of *Kshetra* or Upadhi.

This description of the self of all who is myself is very important because it refutes that self is non-existent or *Sunya* and abstract. Whatever we are experiencing and will experience or already experienced is this self of us. We need to be able to see the unchanging or imperishable in the changing or perishable. We need to be able to feel immortal amid mortality because the truth of all is the self of all who is immortal and not bound by time. All feeling, thinking, sensing, and perceiving gives new experiences now, as the happiness or self is actualized as them.

Keno Upanishad[2] gives the stunning illustration of this self-actualization as various powers and the world: like a flash of lightning in the sky and like all thought processes or mind, determinations, desire, etc. The self of all is really adjunct-less, but appears as adjuncts.

This knowledge of the self of all changes the way we look at other human beings and the environment. Other human beings and the environment now appear to us as kith and kin. Because of this new vision of self of all, the critical security problems and taking advantage of others erase automatically. Because everyone is the self alone, man against man, man against the environment, relationship problems are already resolved.

---

1. 13.13,14
2. 4.4,5

Chapter Twenty-Six

DIGESTING THE KNOWLEDGE

One question that generally comes up about self-knowledge is how to digest it? We seem to understand it, but it remains abstract to us. We understand it, but cannot experience it or our feeling does not obey this understanding. This is a very common question raised by most of us. Then, we stop paying much attention to it and close the door of freedom for ourselves.

We need to be able to digest this knowledge. In order to gain any type of knowledge, we need to commit to that knowledge. For example, for learning medicine, I need to commit to that discipline of knowledge for several years. To digest self-knowledge, we require some discipline and commitment within ourselves. Let us discuss briefly the values that define the seeker of self-knowledge.

Bhagavad Gita[1] describes these values which need to be cultivated by the seeker of self-knowledge in order to digest this knowledge. One needs to create dispassion towards running after sense objects. The seeker's intellect needs to be turned within towards *Atma,* or the self, from external sense objects. It means that the seeker knows that sense objects can provide a certain degree of comfort but cannot give immortality and happiness. Locating happiness and safety in objects of senses is a sign of ignorance and not of knowledge. This type of dispassionate mind towards sense objects is a prerequisite to digest self-knowledge. This does not mean that we miss the transactional value of sense objects, but we do not consider them as housing the happiness and security which is the prime need for all of us. This value is called dispassion towards external sense objects or *Vairagyam. Vairagyam* makes the person into a seeker of this knowledge. This inner turning of the intellect towards self requires repeated effort as our intellect naturally bends towards sense objects constantly from the time we wake up until sleep. Once the intellect stays in self, our feelings, actions, and relationships also follow.

The absence of pride is a value that lies in the seeker of self-knowledge. Arrogance, or fat ego, is a sign of ignorance where generally a person assigns exclusive self-importance because of the pride of his accomplishments. This arrogance prevents the person from pursuing the highest self of him, which is the self of all.

The seeker must be able to see the defects of birth, death, and disease and become determined to pursue a life that is free from these defects. Excessive care and too much attachment towards the family and friends becomes a problem to pursue the highest self. Love and care are necessary towards family and friends, but it should not become an emotional burden for a seeker of self-knowledge. Also, too much attachment to the house and wealth stops us from looking in the direction of our growth.

The seeker of this knowledge should have the highest priority of pursuing this knowledge compared to other things that need to be done. The seeker should train his mind to be composed in the face of desirable or undesirable situations. Evenness of mind is necessary for pursuing self-knowledge. If the mind gets easily disturbed when something desirable or undesirable happens, steady progress is impossible with such an unstable and agitated mind. The seeker's mind should cultivate composure and cheerfulness by creating trust in Ishvara as expected and unexpected situations will arise.

Total commitment and love for Ishvara is necessary for a seeker of self-knowledge. *Bhagavad Gita*[2] declares such seekers should have unswerving and whole-hearted commitment towards this knowledge. The seeker should cultivate the respect and the love for Ishvara. The seeker should turn in as a devotee, *Jignasu Bhakta,* of Ishvara. Such a seeker should practice self-inquiry regularly with the help of Vedant or *Shruti* and Guru. Self-inquiry includes *Shravanam* or regular listening to Vedant discourses or reading texts of *Shruti, Manan* or reflecting on what is heard or read, and doing *Nididhyasana* or meditation. The seeker of self-knowledge always keeps in the front of his mind that the fruit of this knowledge is liberation and the human being's ultimate well-being.

Bhagavad Gita[3] lists the important values of the seeker leading to the self-knowledge. Humility, unpretentiousness, noninjury, forbearance, uprightness, service to teacher, purity, steadiness and self-control are the values which are precursors of self-knowledge.

---

1. 13.8,9,11
2. 13.10,11
3. 13.7

Chapter Twenty-Seven

SHIFTING ONESELF

$\mathcal{T}$he pole vault is a sport where a person jumps over an obstacle or bar using a long flexible pole. Shifting oneself using the practices of Vedant is like the sport of pole-vaulting. Figuratively, we can say that Jiva's identity needs to be lifted to his true or highest identity by crossing the fence of self-ignorance or *Avidya* using the practice of self-inquiry comprising of listening, reflecting, and contemplating on the self. Once the fence of self-ignorance or Avidya is crossed, one becomes free of *Samsara* or the cycle of birth and death.

The shift of oneself occurs when the conscious being recognizes itself in the form of self-recognition. Nothing is mystical about this process of shifting oneself or awakening. It is the washing away of ignorance about the nature of the self through the analysis of Vedantic sentences or

Vedant Vakya Vichar. As a result, the self shines by itself as the self-shining, self-existing, and self-satisfying entity.

In the process of awakening, one is the only friend of oneself. It is like, if I want to appease my hunger, I need to eat. Anybody else eating can't appease my hunger and make me appeased. *Bhagavad Gita*[1] declares that one needs to make one's mind-body as one's friend and raise oneself by oneself rather than putting them down where they can act as one's enemy in one's progress. This implies making one's mind and body conducive to one's ultimate welfare. One's mind-body must become the best vehicle to shift oneself. One should not be distracted and keep pursuing objects of mind-body as the goal of his life. In life, if the sole busy pursuit is to maintain and acquire various objects of the mind-body and senses, then that is the biggest delusion of one's life and needs to be avoided. In other words, one should understand the importance of the human body and mind and make them ready by removing self-negating tendencies like attachment, aversion, anger, envy, and delusion. One should adorn one's personality with qualities like non-violence, compassion, service, love, understanding others, and forgiveness. In summation, one should develop a virtuous and loving human character with a given mind-body. One feels responsible for himself and does not neglect his duties towards others. This type of personality is dynamic and has a strong desire to live with the full potential that human life can provide. Now, one has that boosting power to raise oneself from oneself and pursue higher values in life.

After becoming a highly civilized and social person, one should not remain only a strongly individual person, but see that totality pervades him. Like an ocean pervades a wave, one recognizes that one lives within the order of totality or Ishvara. The world follows the laws or order of Ishvara, including his individuality. It is like a tree rooted in soil and nourished by water becomes aware of its support and sustenance. Likewise, one becomes aware of Ishvara to whom his individuality belongs. This is a shift that occurs in consciousness from the consciousness of an individual to the consciousness of *Bhakta* or devotee of Ishvara. This is where a separate personality of an individual being starts merging to its source.

Bhakta is strongly aware of the presence of Ishvara, or totality, as completely pervading him. A common ground-being of the whole creation is the source, sustenance, and resolution of other beings and *Bhakta* himself. *Bhakta* lives in harmony with the other beings and the environment.

Bhagavad Gita[2] describes the attitude of a Bhakta about Karma. *Bhakta* does his duties as an offering or acts of worship to Ishvara. Performing duties of daily life become a means of worship to Ishvara for a *Bhakta*. He does his duties with the understanding that he is fulfilling the universal needs by doing his duties regarding family, society, country, and world. Bhakta's performance of actions or *Karma* based on devotion to Ishvara becomes his means of recognizing Ishvara or *Karma Yoga*. *Bhakta* surrenders his will to the total will. *Bhakta's* mind-body becomes perfectly in tune with total will and hence becomes the perfect instrument for the manifestation of the total will of Ishvara.

Most of the people stop the inquiry and awakening process after being a responsible and virtuous human being. In this pole vault of human life, half of the jump is already done after being a virtuous human being, but still the bar is high. The identity of a human being is tied with the mind-body creating obstacles in the form of suffering, unstable happiness and peace, insecurity, fear of mortality, sense of wanting, the sense of being little, and wanting love.

A shift of consciousness is needed from this mind-body based identity which is well adorned with human virtues to the Ishvara which is the cause of the universe. Vedant is a powerful pole of self-inquiry to raise us and put us to the other side of the fence of *Avidya* or self-ignorance. To realize the highest goal of life, one needs to invoke the grace of Ishvara through doing actions based on Ishvara's love, regular prayer, and reaching out to help the needy. It is very important to understand that the ultimate goal of the complete fulfillment of human life does not come about without the grace of Ishvara, the grace of the *Shruti,* or Vedant, the teacher of Vedant, or *Guru,* and the readiness of oneself which forms the grace of oneself.

The biggest problem or obstacle of human life is *Avidya* or self-ignorance in attaining the final aim of human life. Due to *Avidya,* which is the ignorance of the nature of the subject, superimpositions are born. Superimposition is of the nature of considering not-self to be the self or *Anatme Atma Mati*. This *Anatme Atma Mati* results in the bondage and suffering of a human being. We consider ourselves to be this limited personality because of the result of superposition rooted in *Avidya* or not knowing the nature of the subject.

The urge of continuous becoming, or *Bhav,* is because of the identification with the ego-idea or *Aham Buddhi*. We have to keep identifying like an actor continuously identifying with the roles, which he plays on the stage. Without knowing the truth of the subject, the resulting superimposition cannot vanish by itself. If the ground of superimposition is not investigated using Vedant, then these continuous identifications and the resulting continuous becoming of Jiva will continue in the form of cycles of birth and death or *Samsara*. To uproot this imperishable tree of the *Samsara,* we need to recognize the nature of the subject in the daylight with no ignorance left. This is described in the *Bhagavad Gita*[3] as to recognize the Atman or the self as Ishvara. Why do we have to keep identifying as a doer and experiencer? The answer is that our identity as the cause of the universe or Ishvara remains hidden for the sake of not investigating it. It is like an actor's identity remains hidden until he knows himself as beyond the actor and on the grounds of which the actor is based. Only and only the knowledge of the truth saves us from superimposition because the superimposition or *Adhyas* is rooted in the darkness around the subject.

The discrimination of the *Kshetrajna* and *Kshetra* makes us aware of our identity as pure consciousness and everything else forms the field of ourselves which is not independent in itself. This realizes our identity or self of a human being as the efficient and material cause of *Kshetra*. *Kshetra* includes the ego-idea. Knowing our identity as the cause of the ego-idea within our own intellect, we stop identifying with this ego-idea or *Aham Pratyay*. The ego-idea is made of ourselves but we are not made of that ego-idea. At the same time, we understand that the ego-idea is like an actor. In other words, we overlay ourselves with this extended temporary shadow of our real identity. Really, this ego-idea or "variable I" is a superimposition upon pure consciousness or *Chaitanya*. It is like an actor is superimposed upon a person. The ego-idea is really a way of looking – an eye of pure consciousness in the form of subject and object division. What happens to us after this realization? We do not anymore suffer from the attributes or limitations of the ego-idea. We do not consider ourselves to be embodied and limited, and as a result, we do not inherit various limitations of the mind-body. Our mind-body based identity falls apart by this revealing of our self or unfoldment of our self as Ishvara.

The whole of suffering is really contained in this identification of ourselves with this limited notion of ourselves as an enjoyer and a doer which depends upon the result of actions getting fulfilled.

Our whole being feels freedom, fulfillment, and immortality which we continually seek. Our thoughts, feelings, breath, or *Pranas,* and perceptions find its source as Ishvara and follow Ishvara. The Jiva wakes up after a long sleep of duality and recognizes, sees, and feels himself without any limitations and sufferings. It is like drying up the ocean of *Samsara* because the continual urge to become something and fulfill some agenda disappears. The *Taittiriya Upanishad* in *Brahmananda Valli*[4] declares that all the desires of Jiva are fulfilled at once.

The finding of oneself to be the fullness or *Ananda* is really the ultimate welfare of a human being. The *Bhagavad Gita*[5] describes such a person as fully satisfied within oneself and whose desire vanishes naturally. This finding of Jiva as *Shiva* or Ishvara completes the sport of pole vaulting between Jiva and *Shiva.* Jiva is recognized as *Shiva* or Ishvara.

One becomes liberated while living or *Jivan Mukta.* The *Bhagavad Gita*[6] describes that such a person attains stable peace and moves around freely without worries about living, free from all desires, devoid of the ego-idea, and ownership idea. This realization of eternal peace, happiness, and immortality is based on the discovery of Jiva that his essence or *Svarup* is the cause of the universe Ishvara, who is the true self of all.

---

1. 6.5,6
2. 18.46
3. 15.3
4. 2.1.1

5. 2.55
6. 2.71

Chapter Twenty-Eight

THE SONG OF THE SELF

*I*shvara is the self of all or *Sarvatma*. The only identity of the whole universe, including animate and inanimate. Vedant realizes the self or *Atma* as the self of all or *Sarvatma* in its full splendor. Then, one can say that "I am" is everything, all, or *Aham Idam Sarvam*. Being the self of everything, nothing is separate or independently exists apart from me.

I am the sun, moon, stars, earth, fire, water, air, space, mind, body, senses, an individual, cosmic intellect or *Mahat*, unmanifest, and all that exists and does not exist. I am of the nature of happiness, truth, and knowledge. I am neither dying nor getting born. I am not subject to decay and disease. I am devoid of anger, hate, attachment, aversion, envy, and cannot be subjected to any mental deformations like loneliness, anxiety, frustrations, and fear. I am disembodied like a sky and limitless peace. I am the imperishable and non-dual self of all.

I am really attribute-less, but wear all attributes. I am without mind, but move as if I have a mind. I am the knower, the process of knowing and known.

I am the enjoyer, enjoyed, and the inspiration of enjoyment. I am the doer, the deeds, and result of deeds. I am space, time, and all objects. I am the waking, dreaming, and sleep states. I am everything, yet nothing is myself. I am *SatChit-Ananda* as myself. I am the mountains, trees, rivers, plants, stones, and the whole immobile creation. I am the creator, destroyer, maintainer, insects, human beings, animals, gods, and the whole mobile creation. I am the common thread of creation and creation itself. I am the seer of all cognitions or *Sarva Sakshi*. I am in the form of knowledge and ignorance. I am the cause and the effect. I am the doer, the enjoyer, hearer, perceiver, eater, feeler, thinker, and desirer. I am is the deed, desire, emotion, food, sound, and thought. Without me, nobody can say "I am", "I exist", and "I do not exist". I am the self of all or *Sarvatma*. I am the peace form and the immortal truth. I am the pure consciousness and the nature of light by which I know myself and the world as myself. Nothing shines before me and is independent of me. I shine as everything. I am the love in all relationships of every kind. I am full or *Purna*. I am the non-dual one who is in the form of multiplicity, diversity, and duality.

Part Four

PRAISE OF SELF-KNOWLEDGE

Chapter Twenty-Nine

SACREDNESS OF SELF-KNOWLEDGE

Self-Knowledge is sacred. It is regarded with the highest reverence by a human being due to its liberating power from *Samsara* or suffering. The sentences of the Shruti become instrumental in creating self-knowledge in man because their words destroy self-ignorance, which gives rise to correct knowledge of a human being's self. Thus, *Shruti* or a non-dual teacher becomes important and occupies a place of respect and commitment for the purpose of liberation of a man from *Samsara*. Self-knowledge is gradually revealed to a human being who uses self-inquiry based on *Shruti*. Due to the continuous commitment to *Shruti*, the meaning generated from its sentences creates self-ward thought, or *Bharamakar Vritti*. After destroying ignorance about oneself, *Bharamakar Vritti* disappears, and self reveals itself as it is. The self shines as *SatChitAnanda*. Self-knowledge is the light of consciousness and hence sacred.

Shruti is revealed knowledge rather than the findings of a human being's limited intellect. When a human being's mind becomes pure, or *Vishudha Sattva,* and ready to receive knowledge, then self-inquiry by a mature mind leads to revealed knowledge of the self as the cause of the universe. Thus, self-knowledge is impersonal knowledge whose author is Ishvara only and hence is considered sacred.

Bhagavad Gita[1] declares this knowledge as the highest secret and kingly. A person may be without any possessions like money, fame, power, skills, and position, but he becomes the king if equipped with this self-knowledge. He does not consider himself any less than others even though he has scanty possessions. Self-knowledge makes one independent of all objects or *Svarat.* Like a precious, one-of-a-kind diamond jewel is handed down from generation to generation in a family holding it secret, self-knowledge is equally sacred, secret, and precious. Self-knowledge is secret because we generally pay attention to the objects of the world and never pay attention to the self because it is closest to ourselves. We do not pay attention to the very self of us because of its proximity.

Self, *Chaitanya,* or consciousness is not visible to a human being's direct or inferential cognitive faculties. It can neither be grasped by the senses of action of a human being.

The whole purpose of *Shruti,* or the systematic knowledge of self, is to destroy the 'not knowing' of the self. Being above regularly available means of human knowledge, self-knowledge is sacred and highly respectable. Self is self-evident and always present. So self-knowledge is irrefutable. Self-knowledge is about the eternal self and hence exists since the beginning of creation.

Self-knowledge is the highest welfare of a human being since it does the ultimate good to all. In other words, it liberates human beings from *Samsara* or repeated birth, death, and cycle of becoming. It makes one experience fullness or *Purnatva* while living. If one forgets where one puts one's gold watch and keeps lamenting, and when somebody reminds one that it is already in one's hand, then one rejoices. Self-knowledge is sacred because it makes a human being eternally happy.

The *Bhagavad Gita*[2] says that nothing in this world is as purifying as self-knowledge. Self-knowledge is sacred because it is the highest purifier. Sins are completely washed off by the touch of self-knowledge. *Bhagavad Gita*[3] says that compared to self-knowledge there is no higher purifier in the world. All previously done actions are burned into the fire of self-knowledge.

Self-knowledge is ultimate. One cannot rise beyond it as nothing lies beyond the self of the universe. Self is *SatChit-Ananda* and is the cause of the universe or Ishvara. One cannot perfect this knowledge derived from *Shruti* sentences any further than this and hence it is sacred.

This non-dual knowledge of self can be passed on. It is handed down to us starting from Ishvara and proceeding from generation to generation of human beings. Let us make ourselves blessed by understanding it as it is for our best welfare and let us keep passing it on to the next generation.

---

1. 9.2
2. 4.38
3. 4.19

Chapter Thirty

PRAISE OF SELF-KNOWLEDGE

S elf-knowledge or *Brahma-Vidya* is revealing to the buddhi of the seeker. Revealing of Self-knowledge transforms the seeker into a seer or a *Rishi*. Who can reveal? Only who is self-revealing. Buddhi can't reveal as only Ishvara is self-revealing. I pray to Ishvara in the form of self-knowledge or *Gyanam Brahma*. Gayatri mantra says let us meditate on the most adored and who deserves the highest respect. Let us meditate on the divine sun, *Deva,* or self-illuminating light to illumine our intellect and to guide our understanding. By the grace of Ishvara and the practice of self-inquiry, self-ignorance is removed and self-knowledge shines.

Who can praise Ishvara in the form of self-knowledge? The only one who knows your glory or *Mahima* can pray to you. I can pray to you because I know your glory. Knowing

you as the infinite and immortal makes me infinite and
immortal.

Ishvara, such is your glory, which turns the finite or
limited like me to infinite or limitless, the mortal like me
to immortal, a seeker like me to whole or *Purna*, the
sorrowful like me to blissful, the fearful like me to fearless, the ignorant like me to enlightened, the afflicted or
samsari like me to peaceful or *Asamsari*, and the little like
me to bigger than the biggest.

Why should I not deify you, Ishvara, in the human form of
Shrinathji as a bookmark to trace back to you, the name-
less and formless me? When your *Maya* covers me, I can
remember you through Shrinathji. When I am lost in
objective experiences of the world or *Lokan*, who wakes me
up or keeps me connected except you *Shrinathji*, my last,
first, and middle resort?

If I start investigating the cause and effect, or *Karya Karana
Viveka*, from the cause or *Karana* of the world or *Karya*,
Ishvara, I end up in the self. If I start investigating the seer
and seen, or *Drk Drsya Viveka*, from the self, it reveals you,
Ishvara, as the cause of the world or *Drsya*. If I start investigating the three states of human experience, or *Avastha-
trya Viveka*, I find you as always present me like removing a
cover from a self-effulgent lamp lighting up the three
states of experience of *Jagrat*, *Svapna*, and *Sushupti*. If I
start investigating the five sheaths, or *Panch Kosha Viveka*,
like recognizing the real identity of an actor, I find you as
the self of all, Ishvara. By inquiring how the mind and the

body functions, I come to understand you as the reality, transcending the subject and the object.

I pray to you as the unknowable, always present, as *SatChitAnanda*, the essence of the knowable mind in the form of knower and known, doer and deed, and eater and eaten. Ishvara, you are the imprisoned splendor in the mind and body, but the prison is made of you. Meaning that you are free in the mind and body. *Jiva* is *Shiva*.

Ishvara, I pray to you not to flatter you with my words, but only because by knowing you one's seeking ends. As *Katha Upanishad*[1] declares, when all desires residing in a man's heart drops, then the mortal becomes immortal and attains Brahman here. Ishvara, as your nature is *Ananda*, the search for happiness of man ends in knowing you. Man seeks happiness at two levels due to *avidya* or self-ignorance. First, man seeks happiness in objects of the world in the form of sensual pleasures. Secondly, happiness is sought in the form of a quest of love in various forms of relationships. Both levels of seeking have the same root of fulfilling oneself from objective experiences. This search for happiness can never end and continues eternally until one turns to you, Ishvara. *Bhagavad Gita*[2] says a man of steady intellect rejoices in the self alone. After knowing you as *Ananda*, still one desires, but to applaud you only, flashing your happiness and peace in relations and objects of the world.

Ishvara, the self of all, the only sorrow-less being or *Vishoka* is you, to whom I pray to remove my sorrow. No grief touches a human being ever after knowing you, the griefless one. The human being is suffering and the suffering needs to be resolved in seeing you as seated in one's heart. As *Chandogya Upanishad*[3] declares *Atmavit Tarati Shokam*. All mental complexes that 'I am suffering', 'I am afflicted,' 'I am depressed,' 'I am anxious,' 'I am lonely,' 'I am small,' 'I am such-and-such,' and 'the world is such-and-such' causing pain, are removed due to its cause, self-ignorance or *Avidya*, being removed by self-knowledge.

Ishvara, I am being bound by the results of actions that I do in the form of merit, or *punya*, and demerit, or *papa*, resulting in pleasure, or *Sukha*, and pain, or *Dukha*. I am the eater of the fruits of my own actions. Who has the power to release me from the bondage of karma except you? By understanding you, Ishvara, the self of all, as myself, one's chain of karma is torn down. Like a caged bird is freed from the cage, one becomes free from karma's binding power. *Bhagavad Gita*[4] declares that one is tainted no more by action and its fruits after knowing the imperishable. All actions end in the knowledge of the self. Ishvara, knowing you as a nondoer self releases me from the unfailing shackle of the law of karma.

Ishvara, it is you that broke the cycle of *Samsara* of action or *Karma*, and enjoyment or *Bhoga*. Before I knew you Ishvara, action, its result, and enjoyment of the result was my fate. Now I enjoy in you as the self and hence there is nothing to do for enjoyment's sake. I found the mine of diamonds as you Ishvara. Why should I look for a single diamond here and there? All efforts of human beings end once we aim at you as our effort's destination. There is nothing left to be done and to be enjoyed after knowing you, Ishvara.

By praying to you and knowing you in the form of self-knowledge, I regain mastery of my own lost kingdom. The freedom that you give makes one fully independent, or *Svarat*, O self of all. Mastery over one's own nature removes all helplessness, obsessions, littleness, and worthlessness.

Ishvara, only you are fearless because you are non-dual. Who else can I pray to remove my always companion that is the feeling of fear? By letting me know that duality is in appearance only, you remove all effects of separateness and otherness that result from it, O Ishvara. As *Taittirīya Upanishad*[5]declares, because a sage sees everywhere his self, he does not fear anything. A sage does not fear even a little due to his vision of Ishvara only. Fearlessness is not possible any other way.

Seeing the unborn and uncreated, or *Sat*, nature of you, Ishvara, mortal becomes immortal. Why don't I commit to you, as you are the immortality that I really want? One becomes mortal by wanting to draw more security and happiness from objects of the world. One becomes immortal by first finding that one wants immortality in the form of security and happiness and second, by turning into the right direction to Ishvara to remove the root cause of self-ignorance. *Katha Upanishad* delineates the story of

Nachiketa to guide us in the path of immortality that all seek.

Ishvara, if you are in the form of self-knowledge, how do I access you? I pray to you in the form of Guru as the remover of self-ignorance or *avidya* that blocks your light like a cloud veils the sun. It is your compassionate guru's form that wakes me up from the sleep of duality. It is your compassion or *Karuna* that takes the form of a Guru.

Ishvara, you are the light of lights, or original light, and totally different from darkness. You are always shining in my heart as self. Nothing can prove you as you are self-proven and self-illuminating.

All other proofs of knowledge including direct perceptions such as seeing, touching, smelling, hearing, and tasting and indirect perceptions like reasoning require you, o light of consciousness, Ishvara, to be proven. Ishvara, the self of all, you are knower and you are known. How can I know you if I am the knower? How can you know me as you are the known?

This identity between you and me, Ishvara, is the culmination of Vedant and every human being's first, last, and middle desire. Ishvara, I invoke you as the identity of all. After attainment of oneness with you Ishvara, the human journey ends, or it is realized that the journey was never started. You are the traveller. You are the path and you are the destination, o Ishvara. It is your love, Ishvara, that appears as creation, which is never separate from you. Your love and knowledge make all the ways of looking at things invalid or insubstantial as you shine as the self of all and the truth of all things. Just like there are many diverse and independent reflections of the sun in a pond but only one sun, as I turn my eyes to you, the self of all, Ishvara, the sun, all reflections are resolved. How can my ego, or *ahankara*, rise on its own as its essential identity is resolved in you Ishvara, the prevader of all or *Vibhum?*

Shiva, you were in the form of Jiva. Victory of life is attained once you, Ishvara, in the form of self-knowledge, destroy the self-ignorance obscuring Jiva, who like a big demon denies its glory from itself. The finding of Jiva as Ishvara and living the glory of Ishvara becomes the new way of life. Let me confess that I was always living in the glory of you Ishvara, but I never knew and hence suffered. Now, I will knowingly live in your glory. The purpose of life is to find you Ishvara, to live in you, and to live as you. A human being accomplishes everything and fulfills himself, or becomes *Krita-Krityah*, after knowing you.

---

1. 2.3.14
2. 2.55
3. 7.1.3
4. 4.14
5. 2.9.1

ABOUT THE AUTHOR

Tushar Choksi is a sincere seeker of the reality of human experience since his childhood days. Due to the undercurrent force of spirituality and the desire to be a good human, he practiced meditation and studied Vedantic scriptures for more than twenty-five years. During his life, he studied in-depth and participated in various activities based on the Vedantic tradition. One major activity he has been part of for most of his life is the activity of *Swadhyay* inspired by *Pujya Padurang Shastri Athavale*. He was also engrossed in the teachings of *Shri Ramkrishna and Vivekananda* and the tradition of *Arsha Vidya* of *Swami Dayananda Saraswati*. Currently, Tushar conducts classes on Vedant and continues his study of Vedant.

CPSIA information can be obtained
at www.ICGtesting.com
Printed in the USA
FSHW021904100921
84630FS

9 781737 397618